CONTENTS

INTRODUCTION

The success of a website can be measured by the results that it achieves. Far too often though, the look and capability of websites simply overwhelm the true purpose of the site, and leave visitors unimpressed. So while people may be visiting in their droves, they're also leaving never to return just as quickly. There are only two things that determine whether a website succeeds or fails. They are:

1. **Visits**: the number of visits to your website.
2. **Conversion rate**: the percentage of these visits that turn into a purchase or an enquiry.

The key to having a successful website really is as simple as getting these two factors right. If you have a website that is not achieving anything for you, then it is almost certain that the website will be failing because of one (or both) of these areas. This book gives you a step by step guide to follow to make sure your website will be successful.

This guide takes you through an easy to follow process of identifying who your market is, what they are looking for from your site and then extends the journey to developing a website that has form, function and is highly attractive to your customers.

The marketing aspects of a good website are well covered in this book, ensuring that the reader follows the simple rules of targeting, consistency of brand, and easy navigation that customers need. There are clear messages about how best to convey the critical information that customers seek from websites, with straightforward planning guides that are easy and practical to use.

In order to develop a highly persuasive website, we will go through four different phases:
1. The Strategy Development Phase
2. The Website Planning Phase
3. The Content Creation Phase
4. The Test, Measure and Tune Phase

The case studies

In order to clearly illustrate the concepts presented in this book we will follow the experiences of two companies in building a successful website, so as to outline the best methods you can follow to produce a persuasive website. The two companies have different website requirements and will demonstrate a wide range of steps you can take to improve your site.

Ergonomic Office Furniture

The first example company is Ergonomic Office Furniture, a retailer of office furniture to the commercial market. The business is a new one set up by Belinda Harris. Belinda has more than seven years' experience consulting in ergonomics, and believes there is a real need for an online facility where businesses can get access to highly professional ergonomic office furniture.

Fix-It Plumbers

The second example company is Fix-It Plumbers, a small business that consists of five plumbers. It is owned and operated by Ray Owens who has 23 years of plumbing experience. Fix-It Plumbers has a current website that does very little for the business. Ray is looking for a new website that will introduce the company's services and generate strong qualified leads for the business.

You will notice that Ergonomic Office Furniture is a product-based company that is looking to use its website primarily to make sales. Fix-It Plumbing on the other hand, is a service-based company that is looking to use its website to drive leads. Hopefully, as we go, you will be able to see some parallels between these two example businesses and your own organisation.

As we work our way through this book each step will be explained by discussing some basic examples of how you might complete the steps recommended for these two businesses. Please understand that the examples given here are very basic; just enough to clearly illustrate the concept. If you want to follow these steps for your own business we highly recommend that you spend as much time and energy as you can on each of the steps.

PART 1

WHAT MAKES A SUCCESSFUL WEBSITE?

CHAPTER 1

Steps to creating a successful website

What makes a website successful? Essentially what you need is to persuade people to visit your website and then persuade them to use your business. By keeping in mind the two important factors of persuasion and promotion you'll be able to achieve a high conversion rate. Another key step in building a successful website is to constantly measure its success and fine-tune according to these results. In this chapter we'll go through the key concepts behind successful websites before running through the steps you need to take in order to build your website.

WEBSITE SUCCESS FACTORS

Visitors and conversion rates

As we've already said, the success of any commercial website is determined by how many visitors the website receives, and what percentage of those visitors purchase or enquire about the company's products or services.

> **Visitors**: the number of people who come to your website.
>
> **Conversion rate**: the rate at which these visits turn into business.

The following chapters outline the steps you need to take to achieve a high number of visitors accompanied by a high conversion rate, as well as explaining the vital theories which lie behind these steps.

The two 'Ps' of incredible website success

If you really want a website that generates amazing results, you must understand not only the importance of your visitors and conversion rate, but also how to improve these two areas. This brings us to the two 'P's of website success, Promotion and Persuasion.

The amount of people visiting your website (your visitors) is directly determined by your website **promotion**. How effectively is the website being promoted? The more effective the promotion, the more people will visit the website.

The percentage of visitors that are taking action on your website (your conversion rate) is directly determined by your **persuasion,** that is by how persuasive your website is. How effectively is the website persuading its visitors to take action? How effectively is the website persuading its visitors to take the action that the website owner (ie you) wants the visitors to take?

These two things (working together) determine whether a website succeeds or fails. The key points to remember at this stage are that if your website promotion is poor, then very few people will visit your website; but bear in mind if your website is not persuasive, then very few people who do visit will be persuaded to take action. Therefore the most important factor when building your website is persuasion.

Persuasion is the foundation

If you are looking at establishing a new website, the first thing you should be focusing on is persuasion. Many people fall into the trap of focusing on promotion too early. They spend lots of money on promoting their website, and watch in sorrow as the website fails to persuade anyone to buy or show any interest in their products or services.

> Your number one goal as a prospective website owner should be to establish a new website that is extremely persuasive, ie one that persuades lots of visitors to take action, before you focus on promotion.

What will your customers need to be persuaded of?

In order to begin the persuasion process, your potential customers need to answer six questions for themselves about your company and your products:

1. Do I trust you?
2. Do I believe you?
3. Do you understand my needs?
4. What's in it for me?
5. What do you want from me?
6. Is it worth it?

If you have been in business for any length of time, you are probably already familiar with how to answer these questions (they aren't unique to the web) but answering them on a website is different from doing it in the real world. One way to figure out how to answer these questions is to understand your target customer, which we will cover in Chapter 2.

✍️ ACTION POINT

Put yourself in your customer's shoes and ask yourself:

1. Does this website look like it generates serious results for this company?
2. Is this website persuasive?
3. Do I feel an increasing desire to buy from this organisation?
4. Am I persuaded by this website to at least contact the organisation?

Be honest in your answers as they will help you face facts about what really needs to be done to make your website a success.

STEP BY STEP

So how do you go about building a website which can persuade customers to do business with you? We'll now briefly go through the different phases covered in this book which will give you a step by step guide to creating a successful website.

Strategy development

The first step in this process will be to make sure that you have a true understanding of the main objective of your website, the needs of your customers and the benefits they will gain from your products/services. By examining these key issues as well as clarifying your Unique Selling Proposition (USP) you will be able to construct a detailed website strategy; essentially a vision of what you want your website to achieve.

Website planning

Once your strategy is in place you will be able to focus on the technical details of your website; creating a sitemap (a diagram outlining the structure of your website), mapping your conversion pathway (the route visitors will take through the site), and finally deciding your wireframing process (a plan outlining each key page in this route). This will allow you to begin planning the content of your website.

Content creation

Having established the detailed plan for your site we will move on to discuss how to create the content for your website; how to write copy, the web features you can use to catch your customers' attention and to persuade them to use your product/service. This content, along with your website plan, will leave you with a persuasive and successful website.

Testing, measuring and tuning

Finally we'll look at what you need to do once you've created your website; the process of testing and measuring the success of what you've built. You have probably heard the saying, 'if you can't measure it you can't manage it', this is very true for building successful websites. Before you can improve something you need to carefully measure it; only when you know how something is currently performing can you try new initiatives to improve it.

Included alongside the various steps to building a successful website are tips and exercises which will help you to understand the key theories behind these phases and to identify the best model for your website.

QUICK RECAP

Key features of a successful website:
- *You need to have a high number of visitors leading to a high conversion rate.*
- *You need to persuade people to visit your website and use your business. Don't simply promote your website and expect it to be a success.*
- *By monitoring your objectives for your website, your customers' needs and the benefits of your products you'll be well equipped to figure out a strategy to build a truly successful website.*
- *You need to use this strategy to figure out the best technical plan for your website as well as the best form of content.*
- *You need to monitor the success of your website and constantly test, measure and tune your website to convince your customers to do business with you.*

PART 2

BUILDING A SUCCESSFUL WEBSITE

CHAPTER 2

The strategy development phase

Now that you know what you need to make your website a success it's time to develop the strategy you will use to achieve this. Spending time now identifying the main objectives of your website, building customer profiles and identifying your Unique Selling Proposition (USP) will allow you to develop a powerful strategy to persuade any visitor to your website to take action.

The Strategy Development Phase is one of the most important phases in the development of a persuasive website.

Experience has shown that most people who decide to develop a new website like to skip this first part and get straight into the detail of planning their new website. Many people will immediately pull out some paper and start drawing how they want to structure the website. Don't fall into this trap by getting into the detail too early. Make sure you take the time to complete this first phase. Be disciplined, put the effort in and carefully work your way through it first, otherwise your results will suffer. This is the stage where you have to take time to understand the objectives of your business and what your customers really want. If you do this now you'll end up with a more persuasive and successful website.

IDENTIFY YOUR OBJECTIVES

Before you even consider getting a new website, or revamping an old one, you need to know exactly what you wish to achieve. What are your specific objectives?

Most commercial websites have a variety of intentions. For instance, they may help to reinforce a brand, or provide information about your company (as a kind of glorified business-card/brochure). However, most websites have a few major objectives that directly drive revenue.

The two most common objectives in a commercial website are:

1. **To make sales**

   By introducing products and services, and persuading the visitor to purchase the products or services on the website.

2. **To generate enquiries**

   By introducing products and services and persuading the visitor to make an enquiry about the products or services.

Other not so common key objectives may include:

1. **Generating advertising revenue**

   By providing great content or some other service, and then generating advertising revenue by selling advertising space or by using an advertising intermediary (such as Google Adsense or the Yahoo Publisher Network).

2. **Generating referral revenue**

   By providing great content or some other service, and then generating referral revenue by promoting other people's products or services on your website and earning referral fees.

> It is absolutely vital that you are clear about exactly what type of 'business result' you are trying to achieve from your website before you begin planning how it will look.

Q EXAMPLE

To clarify these objectives, let's look at our example companies:

ERGONOMIC OFFICE FURNITURE
The major objective of Ergonomic Office Furniture's website is to **make sales**. *Ideally, the visitors will browse their catalogue of office furniture, understand the benefits of ergonomic furniture and then place an order. Therefore their website falls into the number one most common objective of commercial websites.*

FIX-IT PLUMBERS
The major objective of Fix-It Plumber's website is to **generate enquiries**. *Ideally, Ray wants potential customers to arrive at the website, find out about the company and decide to ask them for a quote to complete a plumbing job. Therefore they fall into the second of the most common objectives of commercial websites.*

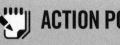 **ACTION POINT**

Try working out what the major objective of your website should be by answering the following questions:

- Do I want this website to generate sales of my product?
- Do I want this website to lead to enquiries from interested customers?
- Do I want to use this website to generate revenue from selling advertising space?
- Do I want to promote other businesses on my website and earn referral fees?

Once you have your answers compare these to your objectives for your business as a whole and decide how to create a website which will suit both.

UNDERSTAND YOUR CUSTOMER

Now that you've identified the main objective you want your website to achieve you can begin to extend this profile by figuring out how to make this objective suit the needs of your customer. Put quite simply, the better you understand your customer the more effectively you will be able to persuade your customer to take action. So often we think we know who we are dealing with when, in fact, we have very little idea. You need to tailor your website to suit your customer or you won't persuade them to turn their visit into a business transaction.

Start to understand your customer by building customer profiles of each of the main types of customers you want to target through your website.

Give your ideal customer a real name, like John or Lucy. Personalising the profile can help you imagine a real customer in your mind.

ACTION POINT

Listed below are a number of customer attributes you will need to work out for each customer profile that you build. Try to be specific in your answers, the more specific you get the better.

- **Age**: How old is he/she?
- **Gender**: Are they male or female?
- **Occupation:** What kind of work do they do? If it's relevant, you may want to analyse in detail the organisation that the customer works for, who they report to and so on.
- **Geographic Location:** Where do your customers live, work, and travel to and from each day?
- **Annual Income:** What sort of income does he/she have, both individual and household average?
- **Skills**: What sort of online skills and abilities, general technical capabilities, etc do they have? Also include particular areas where the customer might lack certain skills. For example, if your typical customer is over 65, he/she is unlikely to be computer savvy, may prefer larger fonts, and need ultra-easy navigation options as well as the standard ones.
- **Likes & Dislikes**: What does the customer like or dislike in relation to a product/service or a website?
- **Internet Access & Computer Setup**: What type of internet access do they have: dial up or broadband? Also consider what kind of computer setup they may have, for example their screen resolution.
  - **Accomplishments**: Any accomplishments or qualifications?
  - **Hobbies & Interests**: Do they have any relevant hobbies or interests? Knowing the customer's hobbies and special interests can assist with promotional targeting.
  - **Networks & Groups**: Do they belong to any networks, clubs or groups?

- **Personality Type**: What kind of person is this customer? For example are they detail oriented, inclined towards loyalty or getting the best deal?
- **Tasks:** What are the typical tasks that they would try to do on your website to satisfy their needs?
- **Needs, Problems or Goals:** This is the most important part of the profile. What are the needs, problems or goals of the customer? In particular, what are their needs, problems or goals that relate to your products and services? What is the urgency associated with those needs, problems or goals – is there an urgent need to satisfy them, or can they wait?

You won't actually 'know' all of the above. But, by visualising your target customer and building a detailed customer profile, you will gain a much clearer understanding of that customer. You will be able to use this new-found understanding of your customer to tailor your messages to appeal to that customer's needs, wants and concerns.

TOP TIPS

Talk to your sales staff and customer service people, as they will often be more 'in-touch' with your customers. Try to find out more about your customers and what they currently want and need from you.

If you don't think that knowing your customer is important, consider this: when presenting your business in the physical world, do you say the same thing to every single customer or prospect, every time? Of course you don't, because good customer-facing people (sales people, customer service staff etc) adapt themselves to each and every customer.

By developing customer profiles for each of the major types of customers you are targeting, you can ensure that your website has been carefully created from the ground up with that customer in mind. And don't worry about the extra time, it will show in your results.

Most websites will end up with between three and six customer profiles. Unless you have full-time staff members who are able to focus 100% of their attention on your website, it is important that you do not end up with too many customer profiles. It is important to remain focused on your most profitable customers. Think of the 80/20 rule here; you want to focus on the 20% of customers who give you 80% of your results.

Here are the customer profiles for each of our case study companies. Remember, in most cases you would have between three and six customer profiles, although in some cases there can be ten or more.

Q EXAMPLE

ERGONOMIC OFFICE FURNITURE
Customer Profile: Jim Taylor
Jim Taylor is 45 and owns a small graphic design company. He has a team of five designers along with three other support staff. They have a loyal client base of approximately 80 companies. The company has a modern office in Birmingham. Jim lives on the outskirts of the city, and so drives through several suburbs daily to get to and from work.

Jim's business has just finished another very successful year, and he would like to upgrade the furniture within the office which is currently tired, dated and worn-out. Jim is not sure exactly what furniture he wants but he does want to give it a fresh and modern flavour and, most importantly, he wants the furniture to be comfortable for his staff and customers.

The organisation has Apple Mac computers with 20" LCD computer screens. The organisation has a shared high-speed broadband connection. Jim is not amazing on a computer, although he does get around the internet. He uses the internet for a lot of research, both personally and for his business – often using it to search for new potential clients He spends most of the time on the internet browsing motor-sport websites, a passionate hobby of his.

Jim has a powerful personality, and likes to make decisions based on clear information. He is not afraid to spend money but wants to make sure he is spending wisely. He also likes to know exactly what makes things work, how the payment options are best suited for his business, and he does not usually make significant purchases without discussing the details with his accountant.

Using this customer profile we can see that Ergonomic Office Furniture need to provide Jim with a website which is easy to navigate and has lots of clear information about their products and payment methods as well as details on the benefits of their products.

FIX-IT PLUMBERS

Customer Profile: Jennifer Simons

Jennifer Simons, aged 35, is the office manager for a medium-sized accounting firm of 42 staff. The company is located in a small building in Whitworth, Lancashire.

Jennifer has an extremely varied role, and she can often be called upon to sort out all manner of problems and complete all sorts of tasks. Amongst her many responsibilities are the resolving of any building maintenance problems such as leaking taps, blocked drains, etc.

She hates dealing with trades-people, as more often than not they don't turn up, or they're late, and that makes her look incompetent.

Jennifer has a modern computer with a 17" LCD screen. The company has a high-speed internet connection. Jennifer is extremely competent on a computer and loves to make purchases online as it is easy, quick and efficient.

Jennifer is a perfectionist and is extremely task-oriented. She thrives on being highly efficient and getting things done, and hates being 'mucked around'.

Using this customer profile Fix-It Plumbers should ensure that their website contains details of the range of services they provide as well as guarantees about the quality of their service. Although Jennifer is confident about using the internet Fix-It Plumbers should make sure that they keep in mind their customers who may not be so technically savvy.

UNDERSTAND YOUR PRODUCTS OR SERVICES

If you are going to develop a highly persuasive website you need to have a very clear understanding of your business.

This is about clearly defining what your products or services are, exactly what the benefits of using your products and services are, and what the benefits of dealing with your business are perceived to be by your customers.

> You need to be able to clearly articulate all of this information to a website visitor to make your website a success.

Features and benefits

A saying which outlines the necessity of this step is 'Customers don't want ¼ inch drill bits ... they want ¼ inch holes'. What this essentially means is that as business people, so often we fall in love with our product or service and think that our customer wants our product or service for the features it offers. But what they are really looking for are the **results** that are offered by our product or service. They want what our product or service does, that is the **benefits**.

Think about the difference between drill bits and drill holes. The person who sells ¼ inch drill bits often thinks the customer is looking to buy a drill bit. But the customer is really looking to get a job done, in this case they are looking to create a hole. This is a subtle but very important difference. It is the difference between benefits and features. Here is the difference: a benefit demonstrates your features (or products or services) being used within your customer's world, so in the case of the drill bits the hole created by the drill bit is the demonstration of your feature being the benefit for your customer.

- A feature is what a product is or has (think: noun).
- A benefit is what a feature (or product or service) does for a customer (think: verb).

It is absolutely vital that you understand customers want benefits, not features.

So how do you work out the benefits of your product or service? Start by listing all your product or service features on a page. Then imagine yourself as one of your target customers (one of the people that you built a customer profile for in the previous steps) and follow the steps below.

ACTION POINT

1. Take each feature and ask yourself, 'So what? What does this feature do for me?'
2. Then try to answer the question (in essence you are trying to work out the benefit of this feature for your customer).
3. Once you have done that ask the question again: 'So what? What does this feature do for me?'
4. Keep repeating the process until you feel you can't go any further.

As you go through these questions you should notice your features slowly but surely start turning into clear benefits for your customer.

If your business sells hundreds of products or services, it may not be possible to go through and work out the features of every single individual product or service. A great example of this is one of our case study businesses, Ergonomic Office Furniture. In this instance it's best to look at the main features that your business offers as a whole (for example types of ergonomic furniture rather than individual chairs etc), and then work out the benefits associated with those features using the method above.

🔍 EXAMPLE

Let's complete this exercise using our case study companies. We will look at three features for each company and work out the associated benefit. In reality, you would complete the exercise with all the major features associated with each company's major product or service .

ERGONOMIC OFFICE FURNITURE
Product/ Service: Adjustable Computer Desks

Ask: *'So what? What does this feature do for me?'*
Answer: *You can customise your desk to your own height. You can sit at your desk, or work standing, and switch easily between the two.*

Ask: *'So what? What does this feature do for me?'*
Answer: *Because you can customise your desk to your height, you and your staff will be more comfortable, happy and productive.*

Ask: *'So what? What does this feature do for me?'*
Answer: *Staff will get more done, they will be happier, and so will serve your customers better.*

Ask: *'So what? What does this feature do for me?'*
Answer: *Costs will decrease and profits will increase. Your business will be more successful.*

Therefore the increase in profits is the benefit of this product for the customer.

Product/ Service: Anti-Fatigue Floor Mats
Ask: *'So what? What does this feature do for me?'*
Answer: *These mats can be put in places where people often stand for long periods of time. They are designed to be more comfortable and to increase circulation.*
Ask: *'So what? What does this feature do for me?'*
Answer: *Staff will become less fatigued from standing in one spot.*

Ask: *'So what? What does this feature do for me?'*
Answer: *Staff will have greater levels of concentration and so*

will make fewer errors, saving the organisation money over time.

Therefore the increased productivity of staff is the benefit of this product for the customer.

Product/ Service: The Ergo Advisory Centre

Ask: *'So what? What does this feature do for me?*

Answer: *The Ergo Advisory Centre contains a number of helpful articles and research papers about the different types of ergonomic furniture available, along with the benefits of using Ergo furniture in the office.*

Ask: *'So what? What does this feature do for me?'*
Answer: *You will be able to find out how to successfully utilise ergonomic furniture within the work place.*

Ask: *'So what? What does this feature do for me?'*
Answer: *Through the successful use of ergonomic furniture you will see an increase in staff happiness, productivity and comfort.*

Ask: *'So what? What does this feature do for me?'*
Answer: *You will increase productivity and save money by getting more done with less. You will also reduce work-related illness and injury, reducing your accident compensation premiums and temporary down-time.*

Therefore the reduction in staff illness and injury is the benefit of this service for the customer.

Fix-It Plumbers

Product/ Service: Upfront Quoting

Ask: *'So what? What does this feature do for me?'*
Answer: *We will tell you exactly how much it will cost to complete the job or fix the problem up front.*

Ask: *'So what? What does this feature do for me?'*
Answer: *You won't get any nasty surprises at a later date.*

Ask: *'So what? What does this feature do for me?'*
Answer: *You will be able to accurately budget for the cost of completing the job or fixing the problem.*

Ask: *'So what? What does this feature do for me?'*
Answer: *Less stress and a more relaxed life.*

Therefore receiving an accurate cost at the beginning of the job is the benefit of this service for the customer.

Product/ Service: Fully Qualified Plumbers
Ask: *'So what? What does this feature do for me?'*
Answer: *All our plumbers are fully qualified and registered.*

Ask: *'So what? What does this feature do for me?'*
Answer: *All our work will comply with local body regulations and British (BSI) building standards.*

Ask: *'So what? What does this feature do for me?'*
Answer: *You will not experience costly and embarrassing mistakes that are discovered by the building inspector at a later date. Problems will be fixed once and for all.*

Ask: *'So what? What does this feature do for me?'*
Answer: *You will save money and will have peace of mind.*

Therefore the guaranteed quality of the work is the benefit of this service for the customer.

Product/ Service: On-Time Guaranteed
Ask: *'So what? What does this feature do for me?'*
Answer: *We turn up when we promise to turn up.*

Ask: *'So what? What does this feature do for me?'*
Answer: *When we say that we will be there we turn up so that you are not left waiting.*

Ask: *'So what? What does this feature do for me?'*
Answer: *You don't end up getting frustrated and wasting your time (and money).*
Therefore the reliability of the service is the benefit of this service for the customer.

These are just a few examples of the benefits which can be identified by examining the major products or services provided.

TOP TIPS

Be as specific as possible with your benefits. For example, if the benefit of a certain feature is that it will save money, state exactly how much money it will save, and provide reputable evidence to support your claims.

UNDERSTAND YOUR UNIQUE SELLING PROPOSITION (USP)

Think about what makes your company and its products and services unique and better than anyone else on the market. Can you explain this to someone? Can you package your product/ service so that it delivers more of what your target customers want and less of what they don't?

One of the most important aspects of the customer profiling process is to carefully establish your customers' needs, problems and goals. What do your customers want to achieve through the use of your product or service?

ACTION POINT

Based on your customer profiles, write some notes on the following:
- What are the most common types of goals your customers want to achieve?
- What are the most common types of problems your customers want to solve?
- What are the most common types of needs your customers want to satisfy?

From these notes try to narrow down the list into the most important goals, problems and needs of your target customers.

Next match up the list of your customers' most common goals, problems and needs with a short list of all the major benefits and features that your products or services would provide to help your target customers achieve their goals, problems or needs.

Your unique selling proposition (USP) should be one of these benefits. Generally, your USP is the benefit that seems to crop up again and again. It should also directly match one of the customers' major problems, goals or needs. If it doesn't, then your USP is very unlikely to attract your target customers.

Summarise your USP into a powerful, motivating phrase, which will be extremely persuasive and compelling to your target customer. Work and rework this phrase.

A really strong USP will contain your strongest benefits, as related directly to your customers' dominant goals, problems and needs.

To check that you understand your customer's goals, problems and needs and the benefits relating to these, try asking some of your existing customers the following question:

'What is the greatest benefit you could possibly receive from using my product or service?'

What they say should match up with your USP and a reasonable majority of the benefits you identified on your list. The case studies below demonstrate how to match customer needs with your products/services and your USP.

Q EXAMPLE

Ergonomic Office Furniture
- **Customer Needs:** *Professional, stylish, comfortable office furniture.*
- **Common Features:** *Adjustable desks, anti-fatigue floor mats and a comprehensive Ergo advisory centre.*
- **Benefits:** *Comfortable and happy staff. Increased staff productivity. Decreased costs and increased profits. Decreased down-time due to work-related illness or accidents.*
- **USP:** *Comfortable, productive and happy staff guaranteed.*

Fix-It Plumbers

- **Customer Needs:** *Plumbing issues fixed.*
- **Common Features:** *Up-front quoting, fully-qualified plumbers, on-time guarantee.*
- **Benefits:** *No stress, no hassle, no wasted time, quick resolution of plumbing problems.*
- **USP:** *Fast, 'no hassle' resolution of your plumbing problems.*

By identifying the relationship between the customers' needs and the products and services offered by the companies, we can see how to come up with a powerful phrase summarising their USP.

UNDERSTAND YOUR COMPETITION

Get to know your competition. Know everything you can about them. Analyse what they do and how they present themselves. Find out their USP and analyse it for points of difference, strengths and weaknesses.

To research your online competition, try searching for your products or services. Limit the search results to pages from your country.

TOP TIPS

The top 10 links listed on the first page of the search engine will often contain your key competitors. If possible, become a customer of the competition or get a friend to become a customer. Analyse exactly how the buying process works with your competitor.

There are a number of free tools available on the web that will enable you to do a thorough analysis of your competitors' websites.

- www.marketleap.com/publinkpop This site allows you to check how many different sites are linking to your competitors' websites. You can also use the same site to check search engine saturation.
- www.zeald.com/Resources/Free+Tools/Meta+Tag+Analyzer. html This site allows you to check what keywords your competitors are targeting in the search engines.
- www.alexa.com/site/download The alexa toolbar allows you to view all sorts of information about any website that you visit. The most valuable aspect of the tool is that it gives you an estimation of website traffic.

If you get to know your competition you will be able to identify the best way to offer your products or services on your website by improving on what is already being done. Like testing your own website you should continually research your competition to create a truly successful website.

DEVELOP A POWERFUL WEBSITE STRATEGY

Now that you have completed all the necessary research defining the main objectives you want your website to achieve and what your USP is it's time to come up with your website strategy. A powerful website strategy is a high-level plan for how you are going to successfully persuade your website visitors to do what you want them to do.

The best way to come up with a powerful website strategy is to pull together a number of people for a brainstorming session.

If you can, it is often a good idea to bring in some external people for this brainstorming session, for example:

1. At least two people who are involved in the business.
2. One person who is a trusted outside adviser.
3. A friendly customer who is very supportive of the business.

The purpose of the brainstorming session is to answer the

following question: 'What are we going to need to do on our website to persuade our website visitors to do what we want them to do?'

Make sure you write every single idea down on a piece of paper. The key to brainstorming is not to worry whether the ideas are sensible or not, and never to be negative about any ideas. Nothing destroys a good 'think-tank' like negativity about the ideas being generated.

Once the brainstorming session is complete you can then go back and carefully discuss the strength of each idea, and start to create a strategy based on the best ones.

It is important that the strategy is not too detailed. You don't want to get into the trap of defining exactly what is going to be on each page (that comes later). At this stage you are just trying to loosely define what you will do on the website to persuade the visitor to take action. Let's take a look at our example companyies' website strategies to see what you should do and what you shouldn't.

Ergonomic Office Furniture

Ergonomic Office Furniture's major website objective is to persuade its website visitors to buy something, either by placing an order directly on the website, or by placing an order with the company through direct contact with a member of the company.

How are they going to accomplish these objectives?
Here is one very common example of a website strategy used by a lot of companies trying to drive online orders:

1. Introduce the company.
2. Encourage the visitor to browse the catalogue of furniture.
3. Present each piece of furniture: show a picture of it and outline the product details, eg what it is made of etc.
4. Present the price.
5. Provide an opportunity for the visitor to purchase.

This is an example of a very typically weak strategy. Why? Simply because there is too much space for the customer to view the product and not get excited about doing business with Ergonomic Office Furniture.

What is needed is a compelling set of information on their website that actually persuades all visitors to take action. They will need to:

1. **Establish their trust and credibility** to convince every visitor that they are a reputable company providing excellent products and great service.

2. **Gain their visitors' interest** by explaining the benefits of working with ergonomic furniture and encourage them to find out more about these benefits by looking through some more information on their website.

3. **Provide lots of weighty information** about each of the individual pieces of ergonomic furniture available on the website, along with the major benefits associated with each bit of furniture.

4. **Demonstrate why it is worth investing** in each piece of furniture from a commercial perspective, and to demonstrate a sensible business case for purchasing by explaining exactly how the visitor will get a return on their investment in ergonomic furniture.

5. **Minimise the risk** of purchasing ergonomic furniture by clearly outlining the warranties on the furniture and their returns policies. There should also be some kind of guarantee to further minimise the risk as much as possible for the prospect.

If this were a real strategy we could take it and develop it a lot further. You should try to ensure your strategy is so powerful that no legitimate prospect is ever going to be able to resist your website's persuasive powers. You'll see some examples of what sort of copy would go onto their website in Chapter 4.

Let's take a look at Fix-It Plumbers, a completely different type of company to see another example of an initial website strategy.

Fix-It Plumbers

Fix-It Plumbers' major website objective is to persuade its website visitors to make an enquiry, either by filling out their 'quote request form' directly on the website or by picking up the phone and calling them.

Here is a website strategy used by many service oriented companies:

1. Introduce the company.
2. Explain what the company does.
3. Encourage the visitor to call the company if they need the services of a plumber.

It's obvious we need to come up with a much stronger strategy than this.

Keeping in mind the key objectives they will need to:

1. **Establish their trust and credibility**: this is especially important in some areas where plumbers have, in the past, gained a negative reputation for service and prices.

2. **Convince their visitors that they are a reputable company with strong values and ethics**: they will need to clearly demonstrate the quality of their team – maybe introduce each of their plumbers, outlining their background, qualifications and special skills. If they are going to convince visitors to deal with their business, their visitors will want to understand the quality of their people. The more information on their plumbers the better – pictures, background, qualifications, customers' recommendations.

3. **Detail their services**: what problems can they fix? What types of work can they complete? They will need to discuss the quality and professionalism of their work and back this up with evidence from customers (ie strong customer feedback, testimonials, awards won for service etc).

4. **Explain the importance of their services: including the emphasis** they place on quoting for all work 'up-front', and in

providing good honest 'straight-up' pricing. They should also detail the focus they have on performing work promptly, and clearly outline their 'on-time' guarantee.

5. **Convince people** to complete their 'quote request form': they should promise that all enquiries will be dealt with promptly and efficiently; maybe even offer a two hour quote guarantee such as 'We guarantee we will get back to you within two hours with a quote, otherwise your first hour will be free!'

Once again, if this was a real strategy it should be developed even further until it was incredibly powerful. You can see a detailed outline of the copy likely to be used by these companies in Chapter 4.

There are a few key points your website strategy should aim to do:

1. Establish the customers' trust and credibility.
2. Gain their interest.
3. Provide lots of clear information about your products or services.
4. Outline your company's dedication to the type of services or products on offer.
5. Demonstrate why they should invest in your product or service.
6. Offer peace of mind by guaranteeing quality of service.

These points should essentially answer the questions your potential customers will ask themselves before taking action (see p.9).

The importance of a good strategy is obvious: there are many situations where one website is outperforming another by a factor of 10 to 1 (or even more), and the major difference between the two websites is simply the strategy.

Now that you have developed your website strategy, you are in a very strong position to start planning an extremely persuasive website.

QUICK RECAP

- *Identify the objectives you want to achieve with your website: is it to generate sales or enquiries?*
- *Build a customer profile to outline the needs, problems and goals of your customers.*
- *Identify the benefits your products or services offer your customers.*
- *Examine your competition to identify your USP.*
- *Develop a website strategy which persuades visitors to your website to take action.*

CHAPTER 3

The website planning phase

You have now successfully completed the preparatory work you need in order to build a highly persuasive website. The next stage is to build a plan that focuses on how you are going to successfully implement your website strategy. You will need to develop a sitemap that includes every page type you feel you will need to make your website successful. This basic sitemap will help your website achieve its objective by making clear the route your visitor will need to take through your website (your conversion pathway) as well as the plan for how each key page should function (known as wireframing).

CREATE THE SITEMAP

A sitemap is a diagram which outlines the structure of a website. It shows the different major sections that are contained within the website, and how they will link together using the main, high-level navigation contained within the website.

Essentially, the sitemap represents a top-down, broad overview of the whole website. It is a very good tool to use when planning a rough structure for the entire website.

Page types

There are many different types of pages that you will find in a website. An outline of the common types of pages is shown below.

The Homepage

This is the first page that appears when a visitor types in your website address and one of the most common points of entry to your website. It needs to spark your visitor's interests and hook them into your website, directing them to the sections they require.

Landing pages

A landing page is a page within your site that a visitor 'lands' on, usually after clicking on an advertisement or some form of link. Most publicly accessible pages on your website could ultimately end up inadvertently being landing pages due to indexing by search engines. Many serious website marketers increase their online advertising results by sending visitors to dedicated landing pages that are optimised for visitors who have responded to the advertisement. This is a great way to test and measure your site, which we'll go into in much more detail in Chapter 4.

Pre-sales pages

Pre-sales pages are designed to help establish your trust and credibility. Using a pre-sales page allows you to provide relevant, quality information to your visitors. This educates your visitor, builds rapport, and demonstrates your knowledge and expertise. The amount of pre-sales pages you will need on a website depends on how much your visitors already know and trust you. A 'cold' visitor will need lots of pre-sales, while a 'warm' visitor will need less. You need to be generous with your information on a pre-sales page. The information you present needs to be relevant and needs to offer something valuable to your visitor. It also needs to be presented in your unique voice. Common examples of pre-sales pages are educational pages, about us pages, customer feedback, and case studies.

Direct sales pages

Direct sales pages are pages completely focused on either selling, or generating a strong lead for, a single product or service. Their objectives are usually to get the visitor to add the product or service to a shopping cart, fill out a customised order form, or register to receive further information. Information on crafting good direct sales pages is included later in the book (see Chapter 4).

Lead generation pages

Lead generation pages are designed to generate new leads for a business. They can range from pages that include basic enquiry forms or contact details for the company, to pages that consist of some kind of offer where you trade free information (free reports, e-books, tools) for contact details (ie you have to register for the free information).

Information pages

Information pages are where you provide supplementary information that some visitors will be looking for. These include things such as your terms of trade, returns policies, privacy policies, and articles about using your products. Make sure these pages are clearly written and easy to understand – avoid using legal terms that will confuse and irritate readers.

Category pages

Category pages are where you list all the products featured within each type of a certain category, for example for Ergonomic Office Furniture's website show a category page would all of the ergonomic chairs they offer. Category pages represent an essential step in the process of browsing products on a website that features a range of products.

Shopping carts

A shopping cart is an integrated piece of software that collects the various products a customer wants to purchase from a website. Shopping carts are used on sites which sell multiple products (or have a catalogue of products), and usually contain a facility for making payment for online purchases.

Check-outs

A check-out manages the actual purchase of products or services by website visitors. They manage payment and delivery details, and generally are used on sites selling multiple products.

Order forms

Order forms are used on sites that sell a single product or only a handful of products or services. Each product/service has a customised and tailored order form.

Your sitemap will incorporate many different types of pages depending on what your objectives are. Use the sitemap as part of your brainstorming tool to further develop your website strategy.

👊 ACTION POINT

Start to create a basic sketch of the different sections you would like to have within the website. Don't limit yourself; let yourself dream and let the creative juices flow.

Think about some of the following when you are sketching your sitemap:

- Customer Feedback/ Testimonials
- Forums
- Portfolio/ Case Studies
- Free Reports
- Handy/ Useful Tools
- Enquiry Forms
- Surveys
- Video Presentations
- Product Builders/ Pickers/ Comparisons
- Product Reviews
- Technical Specifications/ Resources
- Newsletter Signup
- Audio Messages

Once you have your dream sitemap, start dividing the different pages into 'phases': phase 1, phase 2, phase 3 and so on (enclose a 1 or 2 beside each page within brackets to indicate which phase it is in). The essential pages should all be in phase 1, while the more elaborate ideas should fall into the later phases.

TOP TIPS

Don't try to throw everything into phase 1 though. If phase 1 is too big you may never get the website launched. Phase 1 should include absolutely nothing but the things that are essential to implement your website strategy.

Here are some example sitemaps to show how the breakdown of pages can work. Try to follow a similar breakdown for your first attempt at a sitemap to ensure you include all the factors laid out in your strategy.

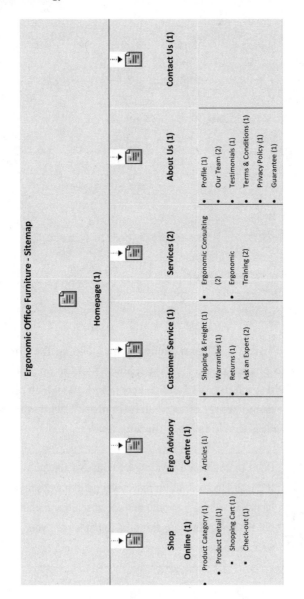

Fix-It Plumbing - Sitemap

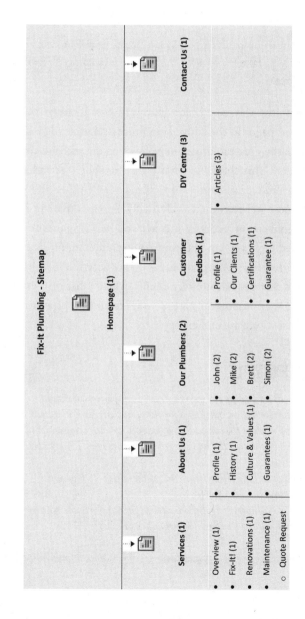

Homepage (1)

Services (1)	About Us (1)	Our Plumbers (2)	Customer Feedback (1)	DIY Centre (3)	Contact Us (1)
• Overview (1)	• Profile (1)	• John (2)	• Profile (1)	• Articles (3)	
• Fix-It! (1)	• History (1)	• Mike (2)	• Our Clients (1)		
• Renovations (1)	• Culture & Values (1)	• Brett (2)	• Certifications (1)		
• Maintenance (1)	• Guarantees (1)	• Simon (2)	• Guarantee (1)		
o Quote Request					

MAP THE CONVERSION PATHWAY

You have now completed your sitemap, a top-down overview of your entire website. It is important that you now use the sitemap to carefully map your conversion pathway.

> The conversion pathway is the path that your website visitors will need to take in order for the website to accomplish its major objectives.

By mapping the conversion pathway, we identify the most important pages in the conversion process: that is, the pages that will have the greatest impact in persuading our website visitors to take action. This shows us what pages we should spend most of our time on.

On most websites there will usually be pages that are not part of the conversion pathway but are still very important as they support the conversion pathway. An example might be pre-sales pages with further information, pages that describe your guarantee or pages that provide contact details. Make a list of these pages as they are an important part of your conversion process and are worthy of your time and energy.

🔍 EXAMPLE

Let's take a look at our two case study companies, and map out the conversion pathways for each company. But first, let's quickly review the conversion objectives for each company and use these to decide the best conversion pathway to achieve these objectives:

Ergonomic Office Furniture: to get the visitor to buy some furniture.

Fix-It Plumbers: to get the visitor to fill out the quote request form or call the company directly.

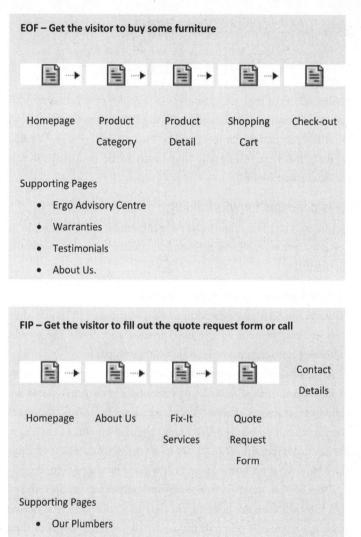

EOF – Get the visitor to buy some furniture

Homepage	Product	Product	Shopping	Check-out
	Category	Detail	Cart	

Supporting Pages
- Ergo Advisory Centre
- Warranties
- Testimonials
- About Us.

FIP – Get the visitor to fill out the quote request form or call

Homepage	About Us	Fix-It	Quote	Contact
		Services	Request	Details
			Form	

Supporting Pages
- Our Plumbers
- Customer Feedback

WIREFRAME YOUR WEB PAGES

Now it's time to start planning the main conversion and supporting pages of your website, a process called 'wireframing'.

'Wireframing' is the process of developing a high-level plan or schematic for each key page in the website, that is the role and features of each page involved in the conversion pathway.

Using wireframing, we complete a simple sketch/diagram of each of the main conversion pages to outline exactly where and what key persuasive elements will be located on the page. We also indicate the type of content that needs to be included in each major content block.

Keys concepts for wireframing

Before we start wireframing, let me introduce you to a couple of key concepts you will need to understand in order to wireframe successfully.

Understanding common user behaviour

How do users behave when they use a web page? What do they look at first? How does the user process and digest the words, pictures, photographs, or diagrams on a web page?

A number of interesting studies have been carried out to try to determine how different users browse a web page. These are called eye tracking studies. These are done by fitting the users with an elaborate headset that tracks the movements of their eyes as they use a website. This allows us to see what users spend their time looking at on a web page, and what they simply ignore.

One of the most well-known and respected studies shows that internet users look in the top left of a web page first before tracking diagonally down to the centre of the page. The user then looks to the right and then back across centre to the left.

What does this mean to you and your wireframing? Well, it gives us some important information about how we should arrange a web page so that people will see what we want them to see.

People look at your website in roughly this order:

1. They look at the top left
2. And scan down to the centre
3. Then they look at the right side
4. Then they look at the left side

Make sure you use this information as your foundation for wire-framing. For more detailed information on eye tracking behaviour uncovered by this research project go to: www.poynterextra.org/et/i.htm

Following the results of these studies we see why so many websites follow a layout like this:

1. In the top left, the logo (the first thing people see).
2. In the centre column of the page, the main content.
3. In the right column, reassuring content such as guarantees.
4. In the left column, links to other related pages (this is the last thing people will see if they haven't been drawn into your content, because it isn't what they were looking for).

Having an understanding of this common user behaviour is a vital feature to keep in mind while planning your website.

Macro-conversion objectives versus micro-actions

We have already discussed the overall objectives of a website. This is what is called the 'macro-conversion objective' of a website.

We have also mapped the basic 'conversion pathway' that each visitor will need to take in order for us to achieve our macro-conversion objective. Each step in the conversion pathway represents a micro-action that we need our visitors to take. Every conversion pathway (and every macro-conversion objective) is made up of a number of micro-actions.

Remember:

- Macro-conversion objectives are the overall objective you want to achieve with your website.
- Micro-actions are every step the visitors take in the conversion pathway to complete the desired action on the website.

When wireframing the main conversion pages of a website, it is important to understand the difference between the features of the conversion pathway, the macro-conversion objective and the micro-actions and their roles in achieving the macro-conversion objective:

- The macro-conversion objective is the main goal (eg to drive online orders).
- The conversion pathway is the pages we need to drive users to complete this objective. (eg Homepage > Product page > Shopping cart).
- The micro-actions are links, buttons or other actions on each page that drive people to the next page in the conversion pathway (eg featured product links on your homepage).

Understanding the individual micro-actions that we want our visitors to take is absolutely vital.

By breaking each macro-conversion objective down into a conversion pathway, and then breaking that down into a number of micro-actions, it provides-clear focus on what we want to persuade our visitor to do at each and every step in the process.

The six questions your visitor needs to answer

There are six questions your visitors will ask themselves, and answering these is the key to persuading your visitors to take action. We have seen these already, but they are important enough that we should look at them again:

1. Do I trust you?
2. Do I believe you?
3. Do you understand my needs?
4. What's in it for me?
5. What do you want from me?
6. Is it worth it?

The first two questions are often mostly answered by what elements you place on the web page. The other four questions need to be addressed by your sales copy and other supporting information, which will be discussed during Chapter 4.

TOP TIPS

As we complete the wireframe, it is often very helpful to keep in mind the six questions that need to be answered to successfully persuade a visitor to take action.

Establishing your trust and credibility

Let's start off now by looking at the first two steps in the visitor persuasion process: 'Do I trust you?' and 'Do I believe you?'

In order to successfully persuade your visitors to take action, you must first establish your trust and credibility with them. If your website visitors don't trust you and believe what you are telling them, they will never buy from you, no matter how amazing your products or services are.

🔍 EXAMPLE

Put yourself in this scenario: as you are walking along the street a man walks up to you. The man is covered in dirt and grime and is wearing tattered and heavily-worn clothing. He smells of alcohol and has the appearance of a person who is living on the street. The man introduces himself as Kyle and points to a brand new Bentley Continental parked on the side of the road. He holds up the car keys and says, 'Sir, this magnificent motor vehicle can be yours right here right now for only £1,000! But only if you pay me £1,000 cash right here, right now.'

Would you pull out your wallet and pay him £1,000 cash? Your response would probably be as follows: first of all you would think 'Why not? The Bentley is worth far more than £1,000. This has got to be the deal of a lifetime!' But you wouldn't buy the car simply because you don't trust him. You probably don't believe that he is telling the truth; in fact he might not even be the owner of the car.

As this situation proves, if you don't establish trust and credibility with your website visitors, you will never persuade them to take action, no matter how good a deal you are offering.

There are many different ways of establishing trust and credibility with your website visitors. Some are influenced by the way your website is designed and built, and some involve the content you put on your website. Let's take a look at some of these factors now:

- **Professional design**

  Your website must not look cheap. First impressions are a vital part of establishing initial trust and credibility with your visitors. Think about the story of Kyle and the brand new Bentley. Kyle's appearance would have greatly affected your perception of him and contributed to your lack of trust in him.

  One of the first impressions a visitor has of your website is the design, the look and the feel. If your website screams 'budget' then it will seriously harm your potential results. Make sure your website has a sharp, professional look. It should look like it has been designed and created by a person with professional website design skills.

- **Website usability**
  Visitors need to be able to navigate quickly to where they want to go. If you confuse your visitors and they get stuck and cannot figure out how to get to your 'Order' page, 'Enquiry' page or 'Check-Out' page, then you will lose their custom.

  The online world is a lot different from the physical world; it is significantly more competitive and does not have any geographical barriers. If a customer is not happy with your service in the physical world, your competitors are probably 20 minutes' drive (or more) away. In the online world, your competitors are only two clicks of the mouse away!

  This is a critical point, your visitors must be able to navigate quickly to wherever they want to go. Your website needs to be very user-friendly and easy to use.

  Many research studies have been completed investigating the best way to lay out a website for ease of use. The theory of website layout is heavily influenced by the eye-tracking studies we looked at earlier. As a result of these research studies, standards have been developed that outline exactly where on a website you should place certain information, and where you should locate navigational menus and buttons and so on (see www.uie.com and www.nngroup.com for more details).

  Think about this: when you go to a website, you know that the company's logo will most likely be located in the top-left corner and that you will be able to navigate the website using either the menu at the top or down the left-hand side. So make it easy for your website visitors by following the same standards that are already being used by millions of other websites. If you don't, you will confuse your visitors and they will question whether you are even a credible business given that your website is so poor.

Think of it this way: what would it be like if every time you jumped in a different car the controls were in a different place. How frustrating! A Bentley can still be better than a Honda without putting the steering wheel in the back seat and the gear stick in the glove-box. Don't make your website a nightmare for your visitors; follow the standards.

- **Website loading time**

Studies have consistently shown, and it is now widely accepted, that if your website takes longer than 8–10 seconds to load on a 56k modem, you run a serious risk of losing your visitor to a competitor's website, and your trust and credibility is damaged.

A good professional website designer should be able to create your website so that it loads quickly. Do not compromise on this point. If they cannot do this for you, then find another designer.

If your website takes a long time to load, it affects the trust and credibility your visitor has with you. It's as simple as that. You can check the loading times of your website by going to www. zeald.com/Resources/Free+Tools/Website+Speed+Checker. html.

Graphics and photos will have the biggest impact on the loading time of your website. Multimedia elements such as animations, audio and video can also have a serious negative affect on your loading times. Text usually makes little or no difference at all to loading times.

TOP TIPS

Optimise your images so they load as quickly as possible. Most graphics programs allow you to do this. If your graphics program doesn't have the required features, you can use the free tool available through the following website: www.zeald.com/Resources/Free+Tools/Image+Optimiser.html.

Trust building elements

So far we have looked at ways that your website can be set up to help you establish trust and credibility. What we have seen to this point are ways to establish your trust and credibility passively: that is through the professionalism of your website design and the general way that it is set up.

It is important that you proactively establish your trust and credibility as well though, even from the minute your visitors hit your landing page. It is worthwhile noting that your first landing page is not necessarily always your homepage. If you have links from other sites or emails, your visitors' first entry to your site may be a 'special information' page.

Specific details will help you establish trust and credibility, including:

- Guarantees
- Testimonials
- References
- Partners and affiliates (borrowed credibility)
- Certifications
- Awards
- Case studies
- Your company profile/history
- Contact details
- A privacy policy
- Terms of trade
- Your client list

Obviously not every company will be able to put all of these on their website, but from this list, ensure you take the time to strategically place some of the elements outlined above on your landing pages and throughout the other pages within your website. Think about what will matter most to your customers, and make sure you include these elements. Depending on your industry, it might be certification, your company history or customer testimonials that most encourage trust.

Pre-selling your way to success

An excellent way to establish trust and credibility is through pre-selling. This is where you give away relevant, quality information to your visitors. To successfully pre-sell, the information you give your visitors must be valuable to them, it must help them achieve what they are looking to achieve.

TOP TIPS

Sometimes a website will contain pages and pages of pre-sales information. This is a good idea, especially if you are dealing with lots of visitors to your website who don't know your company.

In fact, the amount of pre-sales content you need on a website depends on how much your visitors already know you and trust you. A 'cold' visitor will need a lot more pre-sales, while a 'warm' visitor will need a lot less. Some websites have huge sections dedicated to pre-sales information, while others may simply have a paragraph or two on a single page. As a general rule of thumb, the more pre-selling you do the more you will establish your trust and credibility. It's almost impossible to overdo pre-sales.

You must be extremely generous with what you give away at this stage. The information you present needs to be of perceived value and should be presented with your own unique style and flair.

For example, placing helpful articles on your website that assist your potential customers to make an informed purchasing decision can be highly valuable to your visitors. They show that you care and that you are someone who can be trusted.

Putting useful information on your website to demonstrate your expertise is stronger than most sales information you can produce that asserts your knowledge.

🔍 EXAMPLE

Let's say that an accountant who specialises in working with investment property owners wants to demonstrate his or her skills and establish their trust and credibility with their website visitors. An entertaining article detailing some of the many ways that well informed property investors can take advantage of new tax rules can be very effective as a great giveaway, simply because it states clearly that they know their business. This same article could also be turned into a downloadable checklist that is useful immediately to the client, because it makes him or her think about the real issues they need to address.

You may question why any professional service adviser would give away their knowledge for nothing. Consider this: the tiny piece of information offered this way is only a very insignificant part of the whole value a service like this provides. It's a bit like offering up a taste test of ice-cream at the local ice-cream parlour. You know the tasting is really there to help you decide which flavour to buy.

Most people will start looking at your site to gain information. Provide well-written, valuable information, pre-sell to your customer, and you will earn your visitors' respect and trust and greatly increase your chances of persuading them to take action.

THE WIREFRAME PROCESS

Now that you understand some of the concepts behind wireframing your website, we are ready to start putting together the plan for each key page in your website.

A plan is essential to make sure you are achieving the main goal of your website, and to make sure all pages are working together.

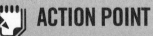 **ACTION POINT**

Sit down with a pencil and paper and sketch out schematically a high-level outline of what you want your pages to contain, but make sure you don't get bogged down in the detail.

Let's take a look at what you need to do to successfully wireframe each of the major pages within your website:

1. Clearly state the overall responsibility of the webpage and state the macro-conversion objective the web page is tied to.

2. Identify how the majority of visitors will arrive at this web page. Will they arrive from another page on your website? Or is this page a landing page?

3. Consider the different content blocks you think should appear on the page. Roughly sketch in their positions. Some of your content blocks will be simple, such as a couple of testimonials, or a client list. In this case write in a simple example of the type of content that might appear there.

4. For each major content block, clearly state the following:

   a. **Target Customer**: state the name of the customer profile the content block is targeting. (Remember the customer profiles you built earlier)

   b. **Description**: create a basic description of what type of content the block needs and what it should say and do.

   c. **Call to Action**: outline what you want the customer to do next (think about your micro-action here).

   d. **Problems/Questions**: Think about exactly what sorts of problems or questions the target customer will have in their mind at this point in the process. Imagine yourself as the customer, and think about what you have just been asked to do. What sort of problems or questions arise for you? Think about what concerns you would want answered before you would be willing to proceed.

Make sure you keep your objectives and strategy in mind when wireframing your website.

Wireframing is most easily understood through an example. Let's develop wireframes for each of our example companies.

On the following pages you will find some basic wireframes for each of the main pages on the conversion pathway.

The following diagrams show examples of the homepage, product category page, product detail page, shopping cart and check out page for Ergonomic Office Furniture. Outlined on each page is the wireframing process for that page including the target customer, call to action, description, problems/ questions and product information necessary at each stage in the conversion pathway.

Ergonomic Office Furniture – Homepage Wireframe

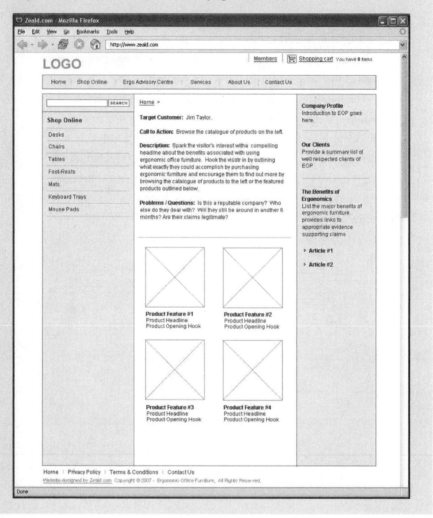

Ergonomic Office Furniture – Product Category Wireframe

Ergonomic Office Furniture – Product Detail Wireframe

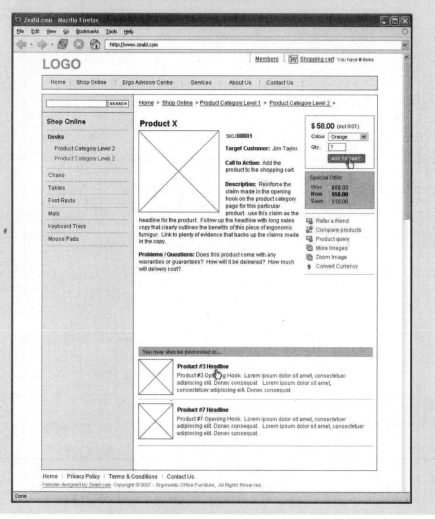

Ergonomic Office Furniture – Shopping Cart

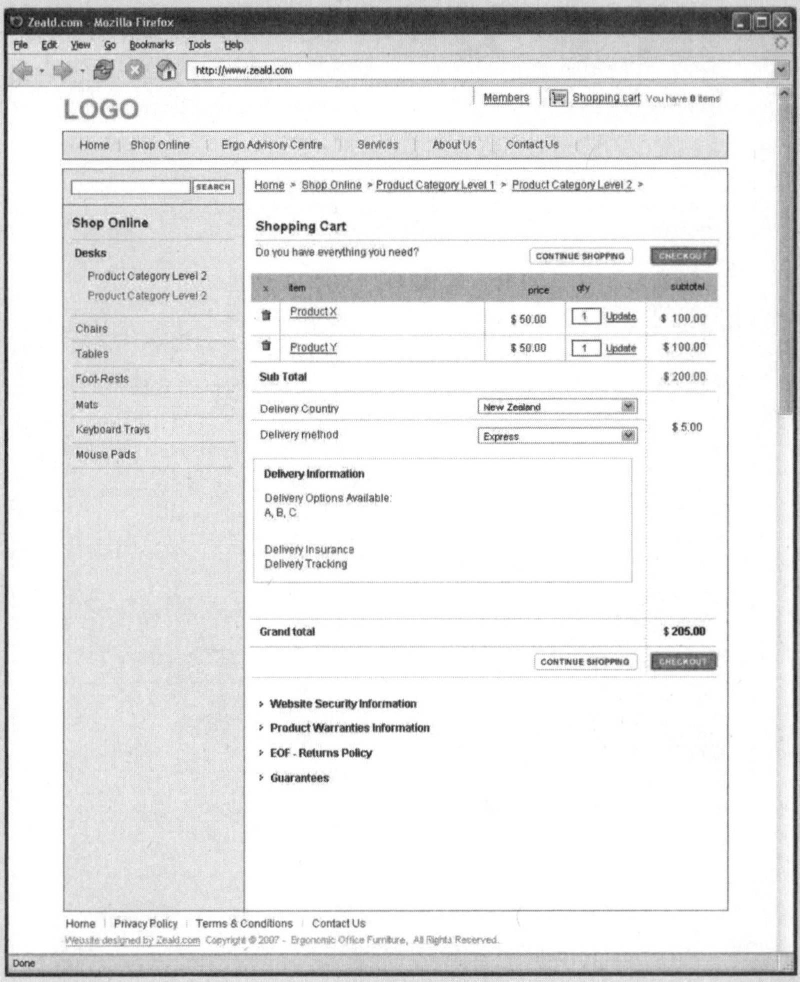

Ergonomic Office Furniture – Check Out

The following diagrams show examples of the homepage, the about us page, the service and the quote request form page for Fix-It Plumbers. Outlined on each page is the wireframing process for that page including the target customer, call to action, description, problems/ questions and product information necessary at each stage in the conversion pathway.

Fix-It Plumbers – Homepage Wireframe

Fix-It Plumbers – About Us Wireframe

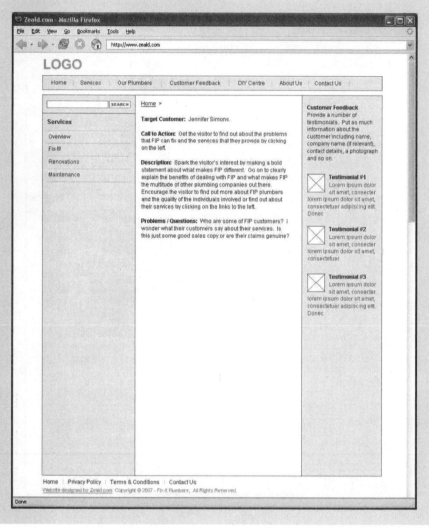

Fix-It Plumbers – Fix-It Services Wireframe

Zeald.com - Mozilla Firefox

File   Edit   View   Go   Bookmarks   Tools   Help

http://www.zeald.com

LOGO

| Home | Services | Our Plumbers | Customer Feedback | DIY Centre | About Us | Contact Us |

SEARCH

Services

Overview

Fix-It!

Renovations

Maintenance

Home >

Target Customer: Jennifer Simons.

Call to Action: Get the visitor to request a quote.

Description: Reinforce the visitor's interest by making another bold statement about what makes FIP different. Craft a long sales letter that does the following:

> Clearly explain the sorts of problems that FIP specialises in fixing.

> Explain the quality and professionalism of FIP works and what FIP does to ensure that their work is high quality.

> Provide some customer feedback to back-up claims about the quality of work.

> Talk about the importance that FIP places on quoting for all work up-front and good honest pricing.

> Clearly outline the 'on-time' guarantee and the importance that FIP places on being on-time.

> Present the 2 hour quote guarantee so that the visitor feels comfortable requesting a quote.

> Summarise about all the benefits and provide a clear call to action.

Problems / Questions: Who are some of FIP customers? I wonder what their customers say about their services. Is this just some good sales copy or are their claims genuine? Will FIP get back to me quickly with a quote.

Home | Privacy Policy | Terms & Conditions | Contact Us

Website designed by Zeald.com Copyright © 2007 - Fix-It Plumbers, All Rights Reserved.

Done

Fix-It Plumbers – Quote Request Form

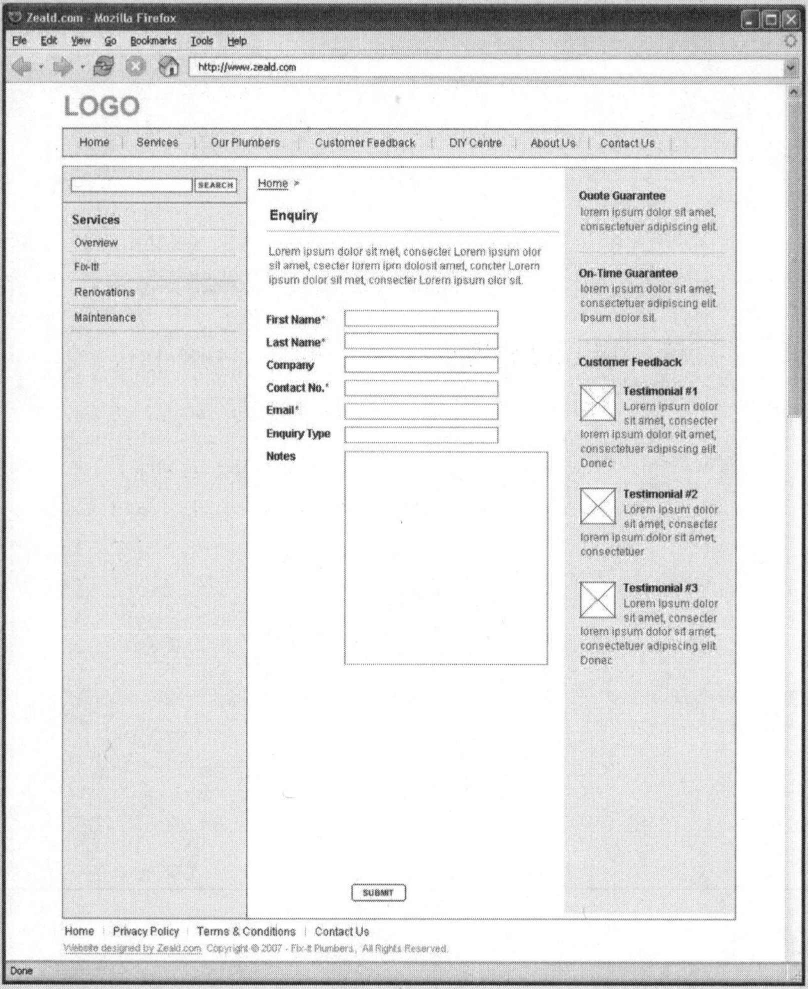

✍ ACTION POINT

Try to follow this wireframe process using your strategy, keeping in mind the key factors about common behaviour, micro-actions and the trust and credibility needed from your customer to draw up a schematic for your website.

QUICK RECAP

- *Create a sitemap, making use of the various types of pages your objective requires.*
- *Map out your conversion pathway, the route visitors will need to take in order for your website to achieve its objective.*
- *Develop your plan for each key page in the pathway, known as wireframing.*
- *Keep in mind key factors which have an impact on your conversion pathway such as common user behaviour and visitor trust.*

CHAPTER 4

The content creation phase

Now that you have decided the technical details of your wireframing and conversion pathway it is time to think about the actual content of your website. The copy that appears on your website is a vital component of what you need to fulfil your website strategy. Good copywriting is 5% inspiration and 95% perspiration, and if you work at it, anyone can write good sales copy and good pre-sales content. In this chapter we'll go through some key elements such as the difference between long copy and short copy and the various features you can employ such as headlines and formatting to help you create a really successful website.

PRE-SALES CONTENT VERSUS SALES COPY

Most highly persuasive websites contain a delicate mixture of pre-sales content and sales copy. Let's take a minute to clearly explore and understand the difference between these.

• Pre-sales content is essentially about building trust and credibility, and establishing rapport with your website visitors.

• Sales copy is about persuading visitors to take action.

Every website has content, but many have little or no pre-sales content. And very few websites have any genuine sales copy.

> A good website needs to have fantastic sales copy supported by great pre-sales content.

LONG COPY AND SHORT COPY

For decades, many direct marketing and advertising greats have used a technique called 'long copy' to achieve incredible results for their clients, that is presenting a longer piece of text convincing the customer to take action.

Conversely website sales copy was originally thought to work best if it was broken up into chunks and presented using individual screens or pages on a website. In theory, this makes the copy easier to understand, and avoids burying the customer in information. This is known as 'short copy'. However, this has since been proven to be a big mistake, because, every time visitors clicked the link to the new screen to get the additional information, a percentage of them were 'lost' due to the 'flow' of the sales process being interrupted. They lost interest and with just a click of the mouse they were gone.

In order to make a buying decision, we need information, and sometimes lots of it. Would you limit your salesperson to the number of words that he or she could use when talking to a potential customer about your product or service? Not in a million years; you would want every member of your sales team to be as comprehensive as possible when it comes to providing your potential customers with all the information required for them to make an informed buying decision.

TOP TIPS

Your website should be representative of the best salesperson in your business, providing all your customers with the same quality, consistent message every time, no matter what.

The way to do this on a website is to use long copy. Try to put all the information your customer needs in order to make a decision on just one page. Use large headings to summarise the structure, so that people can scan through the page to find what they need. This can often mean that the page is very long but it's better than losing a customer.

If you just look at it from a distance this page will probably look like information overload. It will look like a jumble: if you come from a design background you may even think it looks quite ugly. But long copy is what your customer wants. They don't want to scour your website to find out about your products. They want it all on one page so they can read that page and make their decision.

For the reader, having large amounts of text to read is only a problem if the information is useless or uninteresting. If it tells you exactly what you want to know and is presented in a persuasive way, then you really do want it to all be together. For you, the vendor, putting the real guts of the information all on one page gives you the chance to present your sales pitch in the most persuasive manner possible.

Many people are incredibly surprised to find out that long copy outsells short copy. Often people won't believe it is true, and they resist writing long copy or putting long copy on their website, to the great detriment of their results.

> Your customer wants all the information to make an informed decision but you don't want them to lose interest. Remember: Long copy outsells short copy.

Despite this there are, however, a few pages on most websites where you should use short copy instead of long copy. We'll now go through some guidelines to help you decide when to use long copy and when to use short copy.

When to use short copy and when to use long copy

Here are some general rules:

Long copy

1. If you are selling one product or service on your website, use long copy on your homepage.
2. Use long copy on any page focused on a single product or service whenever possible. Provide your visitors with as much information as possible.

Short copy

3. If you are selling more than one product or service on your website, use short copy on your homepage. Highlight a couple of key products or services. Spark people's interest and then direct them through to a page of long copy.
4. Use short copy if you are presenting a list of products or services on a single page (ie a category page). Use the short copy to direct the visitor through to a page of long copy.

In either case, the key to both long and short sales copy is keeping it interesting so people keep reading.

As with all rules, there are some exceptions. But if you are going to break the rules, you should have a good reason, and your reasons should be backed up by solid evidence you have obtained from careful testing.

In most cases, long copy is still the best way to provide information for the customer, so we'll now move on to look at the process of writing effective long sales copy for the web.

AIDA

AIDA, the age-old copywriting success formula stands for:

- **Attention**

  You must get your visitor's attention. This is extremely important on the web, as it is so easy to go elsewhere. One click and 'poof', they're gone. You generally catch your visitor's attention with a strong punchy headline and an 'opening hook', a sentence that is designed to 'hook' the reader into reading the copy.

- **Interest**

  You must immediately arouse your visitor's interest and curiosity. You can do this by telling a story or identifying a problem that your visitor is having (remember to focus on exactly who your target customer is here). Understand the goals of your target customer and identify with them. Pre-selling is often incorporated at this stage, as the information that arouses interest can also be used to reinforce trust and credibility.

- **Desire**

  Create 'desire' in your visitor. This is usually achieved through clear promises that cater to the customer's goals. Focus here on your strongest benefits or your USP and outline them clearly and concisely so they cannot be missed. Maximise your visitor's desire through good, strong 'bonuses' and bold guarantees.

- **Action**

  Finally, finish with a clear 'call to action'. Make it absolutely clear what actions they must do on your website to achieve the desired outcome.

This formula is useful to follow when writing long copy as it helps you to fulfil the strategy you came up with for your website after considering your customers' needs, as well as the key points which we identified your strategy should cover (see p.36 for a reminder of these key points). The following features are things you can employ on your website to help you fulfil your strategy using the AIDA formula.

The Headline ('Attention')

Headlines are the crucial first element of your copy. Their purpose is to grab the attention of your target customer. Remember, everyone will see your headline, and that headline could be the difference between a visitor wanting to find out more and exploring what you have to offer, or just ignoring your page and moving on.

Here are a few ways to approach writing a headline and some examples of each:

- **Promise a major benefit**: Reduce your waistline by two inches in 31 days
- **Offer a solution to a problem:** Learn how to reduce your credit card debt instantly by 30%
- **Flag your target customer:** Attention Homeowners! Reduce your utility bills by over 50%
- **Ask a question**: Have you ever been ripped off by a used-car salesman?
- **Quote a testimonial:** 'Thank you so much! My website sales have increased by 217%!'
- **Sound a warning:** Your air-conditioning unit may be killing you!

Use 'power words' within your headlines. Power words are particular words that convey strong emotions to your readers. Typically they are words that represent something people are looking for. When placed in a sentence they draw your attention. The strongest power word is: **Free**. Some phrases that incorporate the 'free' power word are:

- Sign up today to collect your *free* report!
- Register for our *free* trial

- *Free* gift (worth £19.95) for all new subscribers
- You get our e-book 'Website Fundamentals' *free!*
- Register today for a *free* demonstration
- Sign up today for our *risk-free* offer.

Another effective set of 'power words' is the **How to** phrase. For example:

- **How to** avoid...
- **How to** reduce...
- **How to** save...
- **How to** create...
- **How to** impress...
- **How to** become...
- **How to** generate...

Learn or **Discover** are also great power words, for example:

- *Discover* 10 wealth secrets that every millionaire knows.
- *Learn* the top 32 football coaching techniques used worldwide.
- You will *learn* the secrets used by the UK's top investors, who generate millions of pounds every year.
- *Learn* my 10-point checklist for every property purchase.

TOP TIPS

Here are some other power words that work well in headlines: you, save, know, understand, results, proven, now, today, immediately, money, powerful, trust, create, and secrets.

Try formatting your headlines to attract attention. Use a large font size, with a bold style. Try capitalising the first letter of every word, or put quotation marks around the headline.

ACTION POINT

The best way to come up with a good headline is to brainstorm. Lock yourself in a quiet room, sit down and write out as many headlines as you possibly can. Try to get out 20 or 30. Once you have a good number of options go back through them all and pick out the top three. Review and rewrite each of the top headlines, make them as sharp as possible.

Then test each of the three different headlines for results and keep fine-tuning for maximum success. A good headline will often require lots and lots of reworking.

The Opening Hook ('Attention')

Now that you have caught the attention of your reader through the use of a strong headline, you need to 'hook' your reader and pull them into the main part of your copy.

An opening hook should continue on from where your headline finished. Present a problem, or outline the benefit to your reader in more detail and in a way that they can personally 'identify' with. For example follow the headline 'Have you ever been ripped off by a used-car salesman?' with the opening hook 'Read on to find out about tried and tested methods to ensure you'll never be swindled again'.

By doing this you are more likely to strike a chord with your reader. Why? Because you are demonstrating that you clearly understand their goals, needs and problems.

Sometimes it can be appropriate to emphasise the key points or benefit expressed in the main headline. Give your reader a bit more detail. Try to include the benefits of reading this website thoroughly. If they want to explore and experience what you have to offer, it will be because you've given them a desire to read more.

Headings ('Interest')

Headings are used to summarise blocks of text and paragraphs; you should think of them as being like mini-headlines. Use them to summarise the main points for the accompanying paragraphs of text.

Less is definitely more. These headings are there for one purpose only: to provide your visitor with the means to 'scan' your information, looking down your page to see if there is something that interests them. For example, instead of a heading that says 'A Safe Boat is a Good Boat' cut it back to 'Boat Safety' and let your text do some of the work.

When drafting your copy, regularly review your chosen headings and sub-headings. What they say must enhance the 'scan-ability' of your copy. These vital navigational tools are what many visitors will rely on in their reading, but be careful if you rework the paragraph text below those headings and sub-headings so that they don't become 'out of context'.

Presenting content intended for a website is very different from communicating with your customers on an A4 piece of paper. Some visitors really just want to be able to visually skim your site. They do this by following your headings and sub-headings and highlighted text as visual markers, using them as their 'sign-posts'.

If you have insufficient markers, your audience may become frustrated, bored, or worse, irritated. Your target customers are online in the first place because one of their 'characteristics' as a customer group is that they demand instant information, presented logically, and in a manner that won't hinder their objectives.

You need to make sure your website text makes it easy for them to find the information they want, even without reading every single word of copy. Your headings need to signpost your key points, so that even if it's all they read they still come away with your key sales points.

✎ ACTION POINT

Once you have completed your sales copy, make a list of the headings, by themselves, and put your headline at the top. Review this list to ensure that your headings give readers a clear overview of your message. Ask a friend or colleague to review the list as well.

The Introduction ('Interest')

The purpose of the introduction is to introduce yourself to the reader and establish your credibility. You might use a well-placed testimonial, or select some one-line or partial quotes from your testimonials.

Telling a story is a great way to work an introduction. A well-presented story allows your target market to identify with you. It gives people further confidence that you understand their goals, problems and needs. As mentioned earlier, pre-sales copy is often incorporated here, as it is designed to provide valuable information to the visitor.

Think about how you came to be in the position you are now. What made you offer the products or services that you are offering? Try to share some of your passion to further establish your credibility.

To tell a good story with passion you need to allow some of your personality, or your brand's personality, to shine through. By doing this you help build your customer's trust in you by seeing you and your organisation as real people.

People do business with people they like. By ensuring you are perceived in a likeable and real way, you become more attractive to your target market.

The Body ('Interest')

Do you remember the six questions your visitors will ask?

1. Do I trust you?
2. Do I believe you?
3. Do you understand my needs?
4. What's in it for me?
5. What do you want from me?
6. Is it worth it?

You should have addressed the first two questions on the homepage of your website and in other supporting content pages (About Us pages etc). You will want to further reinforce your trust and credibility in your sales copy many times through further pre-sales information. You can never have too much trust and credibility.

The third question should be addressed in part by your headline and the opening hook where you grab the attention of your customer by demonstrating an understanding of their needs and problems.

In the 'body' section of your sales copy you need to address the fourth question, 'What's in it for me?' The best way to answer this fourth question is by showing benefits. Remember, people do not buy a product/service because of the features. They buy an end-result. They buy what a product/service will do for them.

This is the section where you should use your USP to its full advantage: think back to the list of goals you identified for your target customer, with each of the benefits associated with those goals. This is where you will focus on these benefits.

Use bulleted lists whenever you can. Don't be afraid to really elaborate and give your reader substantial detail but try to keep things as clear as possible.

TOP
TIPS

Your reader is interested in your product/service (which is why they are reading), so give them what they need, and keep it as benefit-focused as possible.

The Offer ('Desire')

Now comes the time to present the offer. Before you do this, please ensure you have done everything possible to make it extremely compelling. Have you created as much 'value' as possible through the presentation of your benefits?

Remind the reader of the goal, problem or need that is being solved/satisfied by your product or service. Summarise the major benefits associated with your offering, and then present your offer.

There are a number of techniques that can be used to make the offer as attractive as possible:

- Demonstrate the value of your offer with the financial benefits or cost-savings that will be obtained through the use of your offering.
- Show a price or offer that is discounted or different from the normal price or offer.
- Compare your offer with that of similar products or services.

Bonuses ('Desire')

If possible, immediately after presenting the offer, present a bonus (or even better a number of bonuses) that you will 'add in for free'. This is not something you absolutely must do, but it will strengthen your offer substantially.

When looking for bonuses, try to find something that has high perceived value to your visitor, but which costs you little. Products or services that have an extremely good margin are generally a good option. Great examples of low-cost bonuses are electronic information products (e-books, 'wallpapers', software, etc). They cost a set amount to create, but then you can distribute them again and again for very little capital outlay.

If you can't think of anything to offer as a bonus, perhaps you are able to provide a discount that is available for a 'strictly limited time'. This also creates urgency, prompting the customer to buy sooner rather than later.

The Guarantee ('Desire')

Remove as much of the risk for your target customers as possible and make sure your sales copy reflects that properly.

Offer the most compelling guarantee you possibly can. As long as you have a great product or service, often the general rule is 'the stronger the guarantee, the fewer claims on that guarantee'.

> A good guarantee will have a huge impact on the amount of sales or enquiries you generate online.

This is one of the most important elements of your sales copy, and one of the fundamentals for your website. People can still be sceptical at times about buying online, and although this attitude is changing, it is important to reassure your buyers as much as possible and remove any perceived risk.

Make a 'song and dance' about your guarantee, as it is a key tool in gaining the trust of your buyers. Remember, the first order is always the hardest. Take a risk with your guarantee, make it compelling. Remember, people are generally honest; it is likely that the extra sales and profits your compelling guarantee generates will hugely outweigh any increases in claims you may have on your guarantee (such as an increase in 'returns' from customers). Besides, if it doesn't work you can always change it.

If you are unable to offer an iron-clad guarantee, because margins are too tight or the product or service is non-returnable for instance, then at least show a stack of top-notch testimonials from happy customers.

The Call to Action ('Action')

Now is the time to complete the persuasion process. When you believe a customer has been convinced they should respond to your offer, move quickly to complete the transaction:

- Summarise what has been outlined in the sales copy.
- Summarise the target customer's goal, need or problem and the proposed solution.
- Summarise the major benefits.
- Spell out to your visitors exactly what they need to do in order to respond to your offer. Give them a firm 'call to action'.

TOP TIPS
Make this call to action as clear as possible. There should be no room for confusion as to what the readers need to do in order to place their order or lodge their enquiry.

Many 'sales' have been lost simply because the seller did not ask for the customer's business. Strange but true, they lost the sale because they did not complete the persuasion process.

Try to provide as many different methods for facilitating the order or enquiry as possible:

- Some people, no matter how good your website security is, will not give their credit card details over the internet. Remove this boundary to completing a sale by offering alternative means of payment, such as cheque, direct credit, money order, and so on.
- Some people would prefer not to buy online at all: provide contact details so these customers can place their order over the phone instead.

The PS ('Action')

The 'PS' is one of the most important parts of a long copy page. Many experts claim that apart from the headline, it is read more often than any other part of your sales copy.

The 'PS' is simply a block of text after you have finished your sales copy and provided all your calls to action, headed with 'PS.'

It's like something you might use in a personal letter or email.
Use a 'PS' to:

- Re-state your offer one last time (and remind the reader of the major benefit of your offering).
- Encourage the reader to 'order' or 'enquire' immediately.
- Sometimes you might even wish to add another key benefit here, as a 'surprise' for your reader.

These small and meaningful portions of text are often heavyweights in that last-minute decision-making process.

SALES COPY OUTLINE

Here is a summary of the different features you can employ in your sales copy to make your website truly successful:

- The Headline
- The Opening Hook
- The Greeting
- The Introduction
- The Body
- The Offer
- Bonuses
- The Guarantee
- The Call to Action
- The Sign Off
- The PS

> Offer your information in a clear and accessible way to demonstrate that you understand your customers' needs and establish your credibility.

FORMATTING

Think about this, when communicating verbally, most people will utilise (and vary) the following elements to make their speech interesting:

- Volume: how loudly or softly they speak.
- Speed: how quickly or slowly they speak.
- Vocabulary: the words they use.
- Personality: the emotions they convey in their voice.

When communicating with the written word, you can also utilise a number of elements that will help make your writing more interesting.

Fonts

Make sure you use a black font on a white background, anything else is difficult to read. Do not use an overly elaborate font. Generally, serif fonts are used for print and sans-serif fonts are used for computer screens. The most common serif font is Times New Roman, while common sans-serif fonts are Arial and Verdana.

Emphasis

Use bold, italics, underline and font colours for emphasis, but use them sparingly. You can also use different font sizes for headings. Tables and borders can be used to frame specific sections of text that you want to highlight. Always use this emphasis to drive home your critical points.

Lots of white space

Use lots of white space. This makes everything easier to read, is more attractive to view and considerably less over whelming.

Vary paragraph lengths

Vary the length of your paragraphs, this helps keep things interesting and means the reader won't lose focus.

Don't justify or centre text

Don't justify text, it just makes it harder to read. Large amounts of centre aligned text are even worse. Make sure your copy is easy to read and just use basic left aligned text.

Graphics

Only include a graphic or illustration if it is relevant and supports what you are talking about. Graphics for the sake of graphics are a waste of time.

REVIEW AND TUNE

Always review your copy and keep on fine-tuning it. Don't keep reinventing it, but regularly sharpen it up. Your copy will be significantly improved by just taking some extra time and care with it. Edit your copy, if you hesitate when reading a phrase, or if you have to read something twice, re-write it.

TOP TIPS

Read the copy out loud to yourself. Even writers with very little skill and experience can quickly spot something that doesn't sound right when it is spoken out loud. Reading your copy out loud is absolutely vital to creating copy that is highly polished.

If you struggle with writing try speaking into a Dictaphone. This can often be a good way to get the creative juices flowing. Or if you are under-confident with your ability to write your own copy, investing in someone who is an expert in this style of writing is well worth considering.

Look at your competitors' websites and you'll notice that a high proportion of them will have very poor sales copy and very poor pre-sales content. In fact, most of them won't have any at all. Quite simply, most businesses put little effort into developing their copy and pre-sales content, and therefore finish with a mediocre result. Either they can't be bothered, or don't know where to start. Most likely you will see a couple of bland, clichéd paragraphs. This is a great opportunity for you to utilise your USP and bypass your competition by having a more persuasive website.

Sales copy and pre-sales content are two of the most commonly underdone areas on a website. If you spend some time in this area, your website will immediately outperform the majority of your competitors.

SALES COPY EXAMPLES

We'll now use the website strategies for our two case study companies to look at the different methods and techniques for using sales copy that we have covered.

ERGONOMIC OFFICE FURNITURE

Headline
Hundreds of office workers require time off due to injury caused by bad seating!
Headline End

Opening hook start
How much are you losing through your chairs? Thousands of pounds, and an increase in accident compensation claims every year – guaranteed!

Every year, business owners are counting additional high costs associated with increased accident compensation claims by staff who require additional time off work due to chairs that cause back pain. The associated loss in productivity is costing most companies thousands of pounds off their bottom line.

Please read for yourself exactly how much this issue could be affecting your own company, and what you can do about it. We know how bad this problem is, and we are totally dedicated to resolving the issue of happy and productive workers for our clients.

Opening hook end

Introduction start

I started this company because I discovered a need for more information and better quality products that are focused on these issues. My name is Belinda Owens, and I have testimonials from so many happy clients that I have total faith in the business I'm in. Let me share with you some insights into why, and the background that led to me give up my physiotherapy practice eight years ago.

Introduction end

Body start

For most of us, getting the products out the door and the money coming in is all we can focus on for at least the first 10 years of being self-employed.

We started out that way too, and understand the frustrations of having critical staff call in sick due to back complaints or being excessively tired. This was my experience while I was running my physiotherapy clinic. Then I started to notice that the most common things which were affecting my business directly were also the most common issues facing my patients. The starting point for all this chaos was traced back to the way they were sitting at their desks, standing for long hours on bad flooring, or tilting their computer screens in such a way that resulted in terrible forearm and neck injuries.

I'm a bit of a terrier when it comes to problems; I like to understand them fully and won't stop working out what the solution is until I'm happy with the outcome. This connection between my own staff being unproductive, ill, or at times leaving because they had to find an alternative job option, and the same issues facing my patients became a bit of an obsession. Eventually I went totally overboard and invested in becoming a preventative cure rather than staying as the ambulance at the bottom of the cliff.

I searched for the best options in office furniture at the most competitive prices so that I could be sure of providing affordable prices for everyone, not only to serve the needs of the corporate level companies who could easily afford the top of the range products. I'm happy to say that most of our clients are small to medium-sized companies who are increasingly recognising the need to keep staff happy and well looked after so that their profitability is not compromised.

As a company we've grown over several years now, with a track record of helping companies like yours to resolve most of the problems associated with staff illness, fatigue, and most importantly, a noticeable reduction in accident compensation claims. What started as a desperate 'end of the road' situation that was highlighted only by medical recommendations has now become a specialised office furniture company that often consults for start-ups and new businesses of all sizes and types. This has been the result of the word slowly spreading about the cost-associated benefits of our products.

You see, we have two clear goals as part of our business strategy:

1. To ensure more companies are investing in good quality ergonomic office furniture.
2. Educating people about the risks of not using this furniture, and the benefits for those who do buy this furniture.

The first part is easy: we have excellent products on offer that have been carefully selected by me personally, with my knowledge as a physiotherapist, ensuring that we are totally confident that the designs we sell will actually do what they are meant to do.

The second part is what I'm most excited about right now, as knowing that you've visited our website looking for the solutions we offer, I understand that you are likely to have a need to consider the reasons why you might be about to invest in products provided by Ergonomic Office Furniture.

One of the things I learned early in this business is that there is an abundance of myths, rumours and general misinformation about ergonomic furniture. For that reason, I set up our Ergo Advisory Centre *(this would be linked on the web page)*, to deal directly with all the mess of mysteries about the industry I'm now in, and this has proved to be such a great idea that we now have other office furniture companies visiting our site and asking to have access to our latest information.

This is something we have been totally focused on. We actively seek out information, and this has led several of us to write articles for medical journals and business magazines about the benefits of investing in ergonomic office furniture such as ours.

Please visit our **Ergo Advisory Centre** to obtain up-to-date, straightforward information about the technical reasons for buying our range of products, and read some of the articles we've had published in recent months.

Or, take action right now, and fill out the online **info-request form** and we'll be in touch with you within the next two days to make a time for one of our highly trained consultants to visit you and discuss your requirements.

Body end

The offer
Let me introduce you to the amazing key products in our range and tell you what they will do for you:

Adjustable Computer Desks
This uniquely adjustable desk enables you to either sit or stand while working. All the components, including screen table, keyboard slider, and the main desk, are fully adjustable.

You can sit at your desk or adjust the height to work standing up, or switch easily between the two, so that you and your staff can work the way you best like to and are most comfortable with, therefore becoming more productive on a day-to-day basis. As an added bonus, your customers will most likely notice the 'extra smile' in their service.

A range of colours are available, and you can *click here* for full details including prices and warranties*.

Anti-Fatigue Floor Mats

If you have employees who must stand for long periods of time, then these mats are ideal for assisting with circulation, lowering fatigue and back or leg strain, ensuring that their concentration remains high, and reducing errors in production. They are especially good for anyone working in manufacturing and retail.

A range of colours, sizes, and shapes are available, please *click here* to view the full range*.

End of offer

BONUS offer

For every desk ordered before the end of September, we're including a bonus ergo-chair at 50% below the Recommended Retail Price.

Extra Bonus – the FREE-Bees

What we know for sure is that our products work to reduce physical stress for our clients' employees. What we also understand is that while our product range is not the most expensive on the market, they do represent a reasonable investment in capital for which the returns may be only slowly evidenced. So, we've come up with a FREE-Bee that will help you to feel even better about making this investment with Ergonomic Office Furniture Ltd:

A **FREE** personal fitting when your desk is delivered for maximum benefit for each person using our furniture.
A **FREE** 24 month warranty on all products we sell.
A **FREE** interest free period of six months when your purchases add up to £2,000 or more.

---

*This link will also take you directly to our shopping cart so that you can complete a purchase online, or you can simply check out our information about each product and then ask for a personal meeting with one of our highly trained consultants at your office to discuss your needs.

Plus a **FREE** Buzzy-Bee Set of Coffee Mugs for your Office just for inviting us to visit and discuss your requirements in June or July

End of bonus offer

Call to action

Don't forget, you can either:

Visit our **Ergo Advisory Centre** to obtain up-to-date, straightforward information about the technical reasons for buying our range of products and read some of the articles we've had published in recent months.

Or, take action right now, and fill out the online *info-request form* and we'll be in touch with you within the next two days to make a time for one of our highly trained consultants to personally visit you and discuss your requirements. *<Online Form: click here now>*.

End of call to action

Testimonials

Here are just a few examples of what people say about us:

'Since investing in new adjustable desks from Ergonomic Office Furniture two years ago, we've had no office staff leave or take extra time off due to health reasons. This has saved us an unimaginable cost in re-training, temporary staff, and everyone seems to get on better in our office too.'

Reg Harrison, Agricultural Finance Specialists

'We didn't really think too much about our office staff when we outfitted the factory 10 years ago, but the need for better facilities for them became apparent within about two years as they began to suffer from RSI injuries regularly. The time spent talking with Belinda was the best thing we could have done, and we soon had a totally different atmosphere in the office every day, with no accident compensation claims last year at all due to RSI.'

Margaret Smith, BEDDCO Ltd

The sign off

I look forward to talking with you about how Ergonomic Office Furniture can help your staff be happier, more productive and less physically stressed by their work environment. I'm totally confident that our products will make a difference to your work results and productivity, and can't wait to add your comments to our growing list of testimonials.

Best regards,

Belinda Owens

End of sign off

PS: if you would rather call me personally to talk about your needs than use the online form, that's fine too. My direct line is 0208 555 5555, and if I'm not available immediately, please leave a message with Melanie (my assistant) and I'll get back to you within one day – I promise.

PS ends

FIX-IT PLUMBERS

Headline

What's worse than having your toilets blocked just before your In-Laws arrive for a dinner party?

Not being able to get a plumber to fix the problem until sometime the next day!

Headline Ends

Opening hook start

There are a million horror stories associated with bad plumbing, and we've heard most of them over the years. Straight away let me assure you that we are totally committed to not contributing to that particular collection of terror tales.

I invite you to read on and discover for yourself exactly how focused we are on solutions that work for all our clients, everyday.

Opening hook end

Introduction start

Hi my name is Ray Harris, and my wife and I are the working directors of Fix-It Plumbers.

I like to introduce my wife, Linda, early on because she's such a big part of the success of this company. You see, when I first met her, she and her friends and family (a family of builders) said things like 'Oh, you're a plumber! Your industry has a terrible reputation for...' They said all sorts of things, mostly related to lousy service.

So, first I convinced her to marry me, and then I listened to all she had to say about how much life would be easier for everyone who needs a plumber if they could find one who actually cared about doing a good job, on-time, and with no confusion about the bill at the end.

Introduction end

Body start

The key objective of most plumbing companies is to turn up, get paid, and leave.

Our major objective is to build a good business that does what our name says we'll do – Fix-It! You see I saw the sense when my wife pointed out that it's important for our own family not to have angry or upset clients calling just before dinner, and taking time with a long list of complaints, that ultimately would just make me moody and hard to be around for the rest of the evening.

I like it when my home life is easy, and that means making sure things like that don't happen. Once I firmly understood that connection, I set about learning from my customers (and doing some additional research with a marketing company) to discover how we could create the kind of plumbing service that not only works hard at solutions for our customers, but was also able to be successful in building up a team of good plumbers who have the same attitude to doing a good job as I do.

Body end

The offer

A few changes were required, we had to learn to think beyond turning up and getting paid.

We know that what you want is this:

- On-time service: for us to be there when we say we will
- Up-front quotes: no surprises at billing time
- Respect for your home: for us to clean up as we go
- A good job done for a fair price.

So here's what we came up with for you:

A Total Commitment to Two and 24 Hour Services

If it's an urgent situation, we'll have someone at your place within two hours – guaranteed. No questions, no being two minutes late, we'll be there. And, we won't interrupt the dinner party in progress either, but just get on with fixing the job, without fuss. Of course, there is an extra charge if it's outside our usual business hours, but not one that will break the bank.

If your situation or job requirement is not urgent, we commit to being there within 24 hours. That's it, we'll tell you the time of our visit when you book us, and then we'll be there.

Up-Front Quoting

Before we start, we'll tell you how much the job is going to be, and that will be the price on the bill at the end of the job. You can even pre-pay the job for an extra 5% discount if you wish.

A Clean Work Attitude

Our team will not enter your home with dirty boots, in fact, they all carry foot covers to make doubly sure there's no trace of our being there. We will take away any rubbish when we finish, and my wife has specially trained all the guys on our team to wipe down the surfaces too.

Our Prices are Competitive – Our Service is the Best

We don't charge extra for doing our work. In fact, you may find that there are less expensive plumbers around, but the work we do is guaranteed to be of excellent quality, and the prices we charge won't have you checking the bank's interest rates on overdraft facilities.

We constantly look for ways to improve on our services, and will give you the opportunity to tell us what we can do better for you after we've completed the work required.

We'd love to have you evaluate Fix-It Plumbers.

End of offer

BONUS offer

Before you call us or complete the online *quote request form* here's a special bonus reason for putting us at the top of your list, no travel charges within 30 miles.

You may wonder why this is for online enquiries only. It's because our management system makes it easier for us to process your request for non-urgent work quotes when you use the *online form* we've provided here, so we'd like to thank you for using the system by offering a no-charge rate for all travel within a 30 mile radius of Birmingham. For big and small jobs this represents a potentially significant saving for you.

End of BONUS offer

Online form – click here now

Testimonials

Here are just a few examples of what people say about us:

'Ray and his team at Fix-It Plumbers saved the day by turning up on time for the work we needed to co-ordinate with the electrician, and even came in at less than the original quote by offering some good suggestions for how we could do some things better on the day.'

Mike, Builder

'We would not build a house without getting Ray Harris in at the planning stage next time. His ideas and follow through on them was legendary; thanks Ray.'

Doreen, Project Manager

Call to action

Please either call us now, and discuss your project, problem and ideas, or use the *online form* provided here for the bonus of no-charge travel on your (local) job, and we'll immediately start to show you how committed we are to showinf that some plumbers are heroes in overalls after all.

ONLINE FORM For Job/Quote Request
Phone 0800-555-5555

We look forward to working with you on your project, and promise to respond to your online request within 24 hours with a personal call to confirm any details we are unsure of, and to make a time to sit down with you and discuss your plans in person.

Call to action ends

PS starts

PS – The 0800 number above is connected to one of our team at all times so that you can rest assured you'll be talking with a 'real person' within moments. We don't subscribe to the endless menu options because we know that if it's important enough for you to call us, it's important that we personally answer your call.

PS ends

TOP TIPS

Once you've finished creating your website make sure to check it works with all available internet browsers, including free downloads such as Firefox. You don't want to spend so long building a fantastic website to lose business simply because your customer can't access your page.

QUICK RECAP

- *Make sure you have the right mix of long copy and short copy to ensure you grab your customer's interest and keep it until the sale is complete.*
- *Follow the AIDA (Attention, Interest, Desire, Action) formula to create the most persuasive content you can.*
- *Make use of features like headlines, offers and guarantees to gain your customer's trust and see the sale through to the end.*
- *Try to review your copy regularly and keep it up to date and interesting.*

CHAPTER 5

The test, measure and tune phase

This is the final and most important phase in the whole process. The Test, Measure and Tune phase is an ongoing process that should never end. In this chapter we'll cover the various kinds of success metrics you can use to value the success of your website, as well as how to be aware of the impact noise and latency can have on your results. We'll also go through some basic testing models and look at the kind of software you need to carry out these tests.

THE IMPORTANCE OF TESTING

If you want to develop a highly persuasive website, you must commit yourself to a system of consistent ongoing improvement, and in order to do this successfully in your company, you will need to follow a Test, Measure, Tune process.

> Every successful website is the result of consistent, ongoing improvement. You should look to make it part of your website culture.

A website is comparable to just about any business. If you set up a new company, it is impossible (even for the most experienced professional) to establish any organisation that runs perfectly from day one. Good businesses become great only through consistent, ongoing improvements. A website is no different. It is impossible to get a website perfect from day one, no matter how good you are. A fantastic website only becomes so through careful measuring and fine tuning.

🔍 REAL LIFE EXAMPLE

John worked as a business consultant in London, and one of his clients owned a car audio business.

One of the first things John investigated was the marketing expenditure of the company. On talking to the owner of the business he discovered that they were spending the majority of their marketing budget on radio advertising. He asked the business owner how many sales resulted from the radio advertising on a weekly basis, and was promptly informed that the business owner had absolutely no idea.

John then implemented a rudimentary measurement system whereby every customer who came to the counter to purchase a product was asked the question, 'How did you hear about us?' The answers to this question were recorded on a simple chart located beside the till. After two weeks of careful measurement both John and the business owner were shocked to find that only two sales had occurred as a result of the radio advertising.

John's first recommendation to the business owner was that they scrap the radio advertising immediately. On further analysis of the results, they also discovered that the majority of the sales over the two-week period had resulted due to the location of the store. People noticed the store on a daily basis because it was located next to a busy street. So John's next recommendation was that they develop some better store signage and put some further effort into their window displays.

The resulting changes made a huge impact on the business, and they all occurred as the result of some simple measurement.

If your objective is to improve website results, you must first carefully measure the different aspects of its performance to discover what is and what isn't working.

The great news is that measurement with a website is much simpler than measurement in the rest of the marketing 'real' world. The invention of the computer has made possible levels of measurement that were only dreamed of by previous generations. On a website, provided you have the right systems, absolutely everything can be automatically tracked and measured by the computer. This is known as tracking website success metrics.

TOP TIPS

A vital process in having a successful website is to ensure there are powerful tracking and measurement systems in place. You should be able to access critical information about the results of your website at the click of a button. If you want to achieve amazing website results, great measurement is absolutely vital.

CONTINUAL ONGOING IMPROVEMENT

One of the unique advantages of an automatic measurement system is that you can test and measure absolutely everything. Nothing needs to be left to chance or guess-work.

Very often people seem to think the key to a successful website is this: you set up a website and then one day you discover a miraculous 'secret' and from that day forward your website performs like a superstar. This is very seldom the case. Every successful website is the result of lots of small, consistent, ongoing improvements, not one inspired step.

If you want to develop an extremely powerful website for your business, you must absolutely commit yourself to a system of consistent, ongoing improvement. You need to be following a continual process of improvement, known as the Test, Measure and Tune (TMT) process.

ACTION POINT

The TMT process is very simple: first come up with an initiative to improve one small part of your website, for this example we'll say changing the headline on one page, then:

1. *Test* this initiative: perhaps by changing the headline for a week.
2. *Measure* the results of the initiative: did the new headline increase the effectiveness of that page?
3. *Tune* your initiative. If it was a success, look to do more of the same. If it was a failure, go back to the old way and try something else.
4. Then do the whole process again.

TMT simply means this: you should be continually testing new initiatives, carefully measuring the results, and then tuning those initiatives to maximise their impact. Keep repeating the whole process again and again.

The TMT method is a very powerful process. Every single successful website is conscientious about continually going through this cycle. It does not always take a huge amount of time; it just requires discipline.

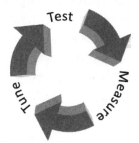

This ongoing improvement will allow you to identify the best model for your website and to be constantly aware of what is working successfully on your website and what isn't.

Remember: TMT: Test, Measure and Tune

CHOOSING A SUCCESS METRIC

In order to TMT your website it is imperative to have a measurable 'success metric' or 'signal'; an objective measure that you can use to know whether you've made something better or worse.

The success metric you will use depends on what area of your website you are specifically wanting to TMT. A list of common success metrics is outlined below.

Visits

The term 'visits' refers to the number of visitors to your website (or an individual page) over a certain period of time. Visits are often further broken down into visits from New Visitors and Returning Visitors. Visits are one of the most common and popular success metrics used by web marketers, especially when measuring the effectiveness of a promotional campaign. The more visits generated by the campaign the more effective it is considered to have been.

However, visits often need to be combined with the next success metric, the conversion rate, to truly determine the overall effectiveness of the promotional campaign. Some campaigns can generate large numbers of visitors but few actual results, as the campaign is targeting the wrong people. Put another way, the visits are of low quality.

Conversion rate (CR)

The conversion rate is the most popular and common of all success metrics. It is calculated by dividing the number of conversions by the number of unique visits and multiplying the result by 100. This is a great way of measuring the persuasiveness (or effectiveness) of a single web page (usually on the conversion pathway), or even an entire website.

It is very important when calculating this that you understand what constitutes a 'conversion', which depends on what you are currently trying to measure. If it is the conversion of the entire website, 'conversion' will be your macro-objective. For some websites that might be an order (as in the case of Ergonomic Office Furniture), a visitor submitting an enquiry form (as in the case of Fix-It Plumbers), registering for a free tool, or signing up to the company e-zine. For others, it could be the number of visitors clicking on the 'Contact Us' page to locate the contact details for a company.

However, if you are doing in-depth TMT you will most likely be trying to measure the conversion at a page level (or micro-action level), ie you will want to measure what percentages of your visitors respond to individual calls to action. Your micro-action might be 'Add Product to Cart', 'Click here to find out more' or any number of other things.

Click through rate (CTR)

The CTR success metric is usually associated with online advertising. It is used to measure both the effectiveness of your online promotions (pay-per-click ads, banner advertisements, text ads, directory listings, email promotions and so on), and the effectiveness of any promotions placed on your site by other advertisers. The CTR is calculated by dividing the total clicks on an item by the total visits to the page(s) that the promotion features on, and multiplying the result by 100.

Page views per visit

Often used to test the effectiveness of website content, this measure outlines how many pages an average visitor views before leaving your website. It is often a good measure of the effectiveness of your pre-sales content, and the overall value of your website to your visitors. The page views per visit success metric is calculated by dividing the total number of page views by the total number of visits.

Revenue per visitor (RPV)

RPV is used by e-commerce websites to measure how effective the website is at getting orders from its visitors. The higher the RPV, the more effective the site is at generating revenue. The RPV is calculated by dividing the total revenue by the total number of visitors.

The diagram below shows examples of some website success metric measurements which illustrate some of the measured signals discussed above.

Website Success Metrics

Last 30 days:

Success Metrics	Actual	Budgeted	Variance
Visits	6313	3000	3313 ↑
New Visitors	4582		
Returning Visitors	1731		
Conversion Rate	7.27%	3.5%	3.77% ↑
New Visitors	4.65%		
Returning Visitors	14.21%		
No. of Sales	459	105	354 ↑
New Visitors	213		
Returning Visitors	246		
Average Sale	$191.63	$120	$74.63 ↑
New Visitors	$171.55		
Returning Visitors	$214.61		
Total Revenue	$89.333.20	$12,600	$76733.20 ↑
New Visitors	$36539.35		
Returning Visitors	$52793.85		

The conversion rate is often the easiest and best success metric to use within your TMT cycles. But, depending on what you are trying to achieve, other success metrics are sometimes more appropriate. Whatever the case, it is important that you choose the right success metric for the job.

UNDERSTANDING NOISE AND LATENCY

When planning your TMT cycles, it is important to understand the concepts of 'noise' and 'latency' and the impact they can have on your TMT cycles. If you do not understand noise and latency, you can end up coming to the wrong conclusions and making the wrong decisions because you have misinterpreted your results.

What is Noise?

'Noise' means any outside factors that impact on, or skew, the results of your test. If you are not careful, noise can cause the results of your test to be incorrect, which in turn will result in you making incorrect decisions.

Examples of noise which might impact the results of your test are given below:

- Natural disasters: a volcano erupting, or a big storm
- Commercial noise: an interest rate rise, a stock market crash
- Promotional noise: major changes in the promotion of your website
- Publicity /Media noise: articles in magazines or newspapers about your industry or organisation
- Competitive noise: a competitor doing something drastic or unusual in their marketing
- Seasonal noise: Christmas, Easter, Mother's Day, etc
- Day of week noise: different results on different days

ACTION POINT

You need to be asking yourself what outside noise could be impacting on the results of this test. Try to answer the following questions:

- Do I need to run the test for a longer period of time?
- Should I keep the length of the test short?
- Should I exclude results from a certain period of time from the overall test?

Use your answers to determine the impact of noise on your results.

What is Latency?

On many occasions visitors will not immediately respond to your offers. Sometimes they will view your offer and then take days, weeks or even months to finally respond. This is called latency. Even the most compelling, low-risk offers have a degree of latency. High-ticket items and complex offers will often have very high latency.

If you are not aware of the latency associated with your tests you can end up coming to the wrong conclusion. Depending on the latency, you will need to continue measuring your results for a period of time after you finish the test to allow the final results to come in.

Understand the 'control'

With any TMT cycle you need to have a 'control', ie the current best version of results, and it is this control that you measure against. Your control sets the standard. Before you set up a test you want to know exactly what results your control produces. You also should know the 'latency' associated with your control.

PLANNING YOUR VARIATIONS OR RECIPES

Once you know your success metric and your control, you are ready to set up your recipes, the combinations of success metrics you have chosen to monitor. These are the variations to the control you want to test. You need to carefully plan your recipes before starting your TMT cycle.

There are an almost unlimited number of things you can TMT, but it makes sense that initially you focus on these elements in your recipes:

1. Headlines
2. Opening Hooks
3. Pictures/Hero Shots
4. Trust-Building Elements

5. Pre-Sales Copy
6. Teasers and Short Copy
7. Bulleted Lists of Benefits or Features
8. Calls to Action
9. Pricing /Your Offers
10. Order Forms /Check-Outs
11. Length of Forms
12. Button & Link Messaging
13. Cross Sells & Up Sells
14. The PS

In addition to testing the different elements outlined above, it is often a good idea to test 'element attributes'. For example, the element might be the headline, but some element attributes might be font size, font colour and so on. Examples of common element attributes are as follows:

• Size
• Alignment
• Style
• Colour
• Background Colour
• Position
• Bold /Italics /Underline

The options are almost endless. Use your intuition here, and create recipes you think are likely to lead to a positive result. Focus first on the elements that appear on the screen without needing to scroll.

HOW TO TEST

There are a number of different ways you can conduct a TMT cycle. Before we look at this though, a very common and valid question is: how long do I need to run my test before I can trust the results? Or how many visitors do I need to have visit each different recipe before I can trust the results of the test?

This is a very difficult question to answer, as it depends on the noise and the difference in the results between the control and the recipe. Good testing software will tell you the 'Confidence Level' that your test has achieved (e.g. 60%, 90%, 95%, 99%). However, if you don't have sophisticated testing software, as a general rule of thumb when working with small businesses it's a good idea to run tests on a 'sample size' of 500 to 1,000 high-quality visitors (quality prospects, not random clickers) before trusting the results.

TOP TIPS

Make sure you use your customer profile to help you carry out your TMT process and make your site even more persuasive.

Let's take a look at the different ways to conduct a TMT cycle.

Basic testing

Basic testing works like this. You run the original version (version A) and then run the proposed new and improved version (version B) and then compare the results of the two different versions (A versus B). This type of testing is better than not testing at all, but it is susceptible to many environmental factors that can skew the results of the test. It is also quite slow and can take a long time to test a number of different elements. Be very careful when you are using basic testing and think through any outside noise that may impact the results of your test. And most importantly of all, make sure you run large sample sizes to keep the confidence level of your tests nice and high.

Split testing

Split testing is where you run both the original version of the test and the new recipe(s) at the same time with half the people viewing the original and half the people viewing the new recipe.

This form of testing is more complicated but minimises the effects of noise. Split testing requires specialised software, but as long as you have it the software is simple to use. There are many different types of split testing software available. A quick search on the internet will bring up many different providers.

Multivariate testing

Multivariate testing is where you test many different variables all at the same time and use sophisticated software and mathematical analysis to work out exactly which combination of variables produces the best results. Multivariate testing allows you to optimise a web page as quickly as possible but it requires powerful software, careful planning and can be very complex to set up. The most widely recognised providers of multivariate testing software are as follows:

- Google Website Optimizer
- Vertster
- Offermatica
- SiteSpect

Testing software

There are many different software packages that measure the performance of a website. Most packages fall under one of two types.

The first type of package analyses the log files produced by the web server that hosts the website. What does this mean? Most web servers record information about the activity that has occurred on the website in a 'log file', that is a file which lists all the actions which have occurred. By analysing this log file, it is possible to retrieve all sorts of information about the visitors that are viewing a website and the pages that they are viewing.

Good log file analysis tools will provide information about:

- The number of visitors
- The amount of times a visitor has viewed a page
- What type of operating system and web browser the visitor was using

- Where the visitor was geographically located
- How the visitor found the website, etc.

However, typically they will provide very little information regarding the 'conversion rate' and other important success metrics. This effectively makes them inadequate for anyone who is serious about TMT and improving their website results.

The other common type of measurement packages require reporting code to be inserted into each and every web page on the website. The reporting code enables all sorts of extra information to be recorded about the visitor and their interaction with the website. Inserting the reporting code is a technical task and although it requires some technical skills and expertise it does provide a far more comprehensive array of information.

Most web hosting providers will provide a free website measurement package that analyses the log files of the website. But to seriously perform TMT on your website you will need to have a comprehensive measurement system built into the website. More and more website designers are starting to realise the importance of measurement and are building websites with a measurement system included as part of the website. The cost of measurement systems range from a free service through to many thousands of pounds per year.

Probably the most popular low-cost system is one provided by Google called 'Google Analytics'. Google Analytics is provided free of charge. It is a sophisticated system that provides all sorts of useful reports. However Google does reserve the right to utilise your information in various different ways. Other popular measurement systems include: Nedstat, ClickTracks, Omniture, SageMetrics, and WebTrends.

QUICK RECAP

- *Make sure you consistently test your website to check you are achieving your objective.*
- *Decide on the type of success metric you will need to monitor various parts of your website, be it the number of visitors, the conversion rate or revenue per visitor.*
- *Ensure you keep factors such as noise and latency in mind and monitor the results of your control against the results you want to see.*
- *Come up with a range of recipes to test your website, changing factors such as headlines and copy as well as smaller attributes such as font.*
- *Research the various kinds of tests you can run and the types of measuring software available to help you continue your process of TMT.*

CONCLUSION

Now that you've followed each of the steps outlined in this book you will have learnt some valuable skills and techniques to apply to building your website which will make an incredible difference to its performance and success.

Just remember some of the key points we've covered throughout the guide:

- You need to have a clear website objective to persuade visitors to take action.
- Spend time building this objective and strategy by focusing on your customers' needs, the benefits of your products/ services and your USP.
- Use this information to build your sitemap and conversion pathways and come up with a great wireframing process for the key pages in your website.
- Make sure the content of your website is a good mix of long and short copy and employs useful features such as headlines, opening hooks, bonuses and guarantees to see a sale through to the end.
- Once your website is up and running, implement an ongoing process of Test, Measure, Tune to make sure your website is as successful as it can be.

You can have the best information in the world, but if you do not act on that information then you will never achieve an amazing result. Follow the steps in this guide and you'll be well on your way to building a persuasive and successful website.

QUICKSTART GUIDE

Summary of key points

CHAPTER 01: KEYS STEPS TO CREATING A SUCCESSFUL WEBSITE

- You need to have a high number of visitors leading to a high conversion rate.
- You need to persuade people to visit your website and use your business. Don't simply promote your website and expect it to be a success.
- By monitoring your objectives for your website, your customers' needs and the benefits of your products, you'll be well equipped to figure out a strategy to build a truly successful website.
- You need to use this strategy to figure out the best technical plan for your website as well as the best form of content.
- You need to monitor the success of your website and constantly test, measure and tune your website to convince your customers to do business with you.

CHAPTER 02: THE STRATEGY DEVELOPMENT PHASE

- Identify the objectives you want to achieve with your website: is it to generate sales or enquiries?
- Build a customer profile to outline the needs, problems and goals of your customers.
- Identify the benefits your products or services offer your customers.
- Examine your competition to identify your USP.
- Develop a website strategy which persuades visitors to your website to take action.

CHAPTER 03: THE WEBSITE PLANNING PHASE

- Create a sitemap, making use of the various types of pages your objective requires.
- Map out your conversion pathway, the route visitors will need to take in order for your website to achieve its objective.
- Develop your plan for each key page in the pathway, known as wireframing.
- Keep in mind key factors which have an impact on your conversion pathway such as common user behaviour and visitor trust.

CHAPTER 04: THE CONTENT CREATION PHASE

- Make sure you have the right mix of long copy and short copy to ensure you grab your customer's interest but keep it until the sale is complete.
- Follow the AIDA (Attention, Interest, Desire, Action) formula to create the most persuasive content you can.
- Make use of features like headlines, offers and guarantees to gain your customer's trust and see the sale through to the end.
- Try to review your copy regularly and keep it up to date and interesting.

CHAPTER 05: THE TEST, MEASURE AND TUNE PHASE

- Make sure you consistently test your website to check you are achieving your objective.

- Decide on the type of success metric you will need to monitor various parts of your website, be it number of visitors, the conversion rate or revenue per visitor.

- Ensure you keep factors such as noise and latency in mind and monitor the results of your control against the results you want to see.

- Come up with a range of recipes to test your website, changing factors such as headlines and copy as well as smaller attributes such as font.

- Research the various kinds of tests you can run and the types of measuring software available to help you continue your process of TMT.

Index